A
COLLECTION
OF WELSH
TRAVELS,
AND
Memoirs of *WALES*

CONTAINING

The whole collected by John Torbuck
a mighty Lover of *Welsh* Travels

London
Spradabach Publishing
2022

Hounskull Publishing
BM Box Hounskull
London WC1N 3XX

A Collection of Welsh Travels and Memoirs of Wales
Originally published in 1740
First Hounskull edition published 2022
© Hounskull Publishing 2022

ISBN 978-1-910893-11-1

British Library Cataloguing-in-Publication Data:
A catalogue record for this book is available from the British Library.

Table of Contents

Note on This Edition

The text in this volume is based on the 1738, 1742, 1743, and 1748 editions printed in Dublin by John Torbuck. The punctuation and spelling are as in the original, except the archaic long 's' has been replaced by the modern short 's'. Capitalisation follows the 1748 edition. Place names composed of two words, have been rendered in the modern fashion, removing the hyphen and capitalising both words.

A number of editorial footnotes have been added and identified as such.

An index has been generated.

The Briton Described, or a Journey Thro' Wales

To
Sir Richard Wenman,
of Casswell in the
County of Oxford, Baronet

Sir,

aving had the honour to be employed in a *negotiation* between an *English* Gentleman and the ancient *Britons*, I was not only upon the borders, and (as it were) the Limbs of *Wales*, but have travelled through the very *bowels* of the country; in which journey there did salute me so many *occurrences* worthy of observation, that I could not forbear a description of them, and presenting you with the (as I may say) *Wallography* of my voyage.

I make bold to imitate one *Alexander* of *Greece*, who still, as he went dragooning about the world, described the wandering, and (as it were) the *Tom Coriatism*[1] of his expeditions; only in this I shall differ from him; whereas he gave only a bare *image* and *pourtraiture* of the country, I shall draw the *character* of the *inhabitants*, and shall not only express in a map or table the mere *picture* of the place, and tell you that here *stands* one town, and *twenty* miles off stands another: but my design is to give you a narrative of what I observed concerning the nature of the soil, and of the inhabitants, their original, persons, diet apparel, language, laws, customs, policy, &c.

But what need I go so far as *Macedonia* for a *pattern*, seeing we have so many *precedents* at home? For one tells us in folio, that he hath been at *Constantinople*; another that he hath been at *Vienna*; a third, that he hath been in *Spain*; and why may I not tell the world in *duodecimo*, that I have been in Wales? When a fellow hath either a *maggot* in his pate, or a *breeze* in his tail, that he cannot fix long in a place; or perhaps, when he hath *entitled* himself by some misdemeanours either to the pillory or gibet, to *disinherit* himself of his deserved right, he *flirts* into *Holland*, or is transported into some foreign country; where, conversing little while, he thrusts into the world the history of his adventures, he *varnisheth* over his banishrent,

---

1   Tom Coriat was a whimsical traveller, who, in King James's time, beat upon the hoof about two or three thousand miles, and returned home as very a coxcomb as he went out. See his *Travels call'd his Crudities*.

with the name of travels, and stiles that his *recreation* which was, indeed, his *punishment*, and so *dignifies* a ramble by the name of journey. He tells what *wonderments* have surpriz'd him, what *fragments* of antiquity have amazed him, what structures have ravished him, what hills have tir'd him; in a word, he is *big* with descriptions, and obliges you with the narrative of all his observations and Notices; seeing everyone almost, that hath but *untruss'd* in a foreign country, will have his voyage recorded, and every *Letter-carrier* beyond sea would be thought a *Drake* or a *Cavendish*, I thought with myself, why may not I have the liberty of relating my journey, and of communicating my observations to mankind. I must confess, my *pilgrimage* was not far, but perhaps it was *checquered* with as great variety, both of pleasure and peril, as a longer progress; neither are my remarks very solemn and stately, but yet they were such as gratify'd my curiosity, and pleased my humour as well as the observations of longer journals.

Such as they are (Sir!) I humbly crave leave to devote them to your perusal, as the most signal *testimony* of that venerable *esteem* I have for you, I wave your *panegyrick*, and forbear to rhetoricate, or to *descant* in your praise. You are too *copious* a subject even for the most *transcendent* oratory. I like not to display your personal accomplishments, which are so eminent and conspicuous already in the world. I know an attempt of that nature would be too great a *violence* to your *modesty*, and I am sure too hard a *task* for my *capacity*. My present business (Sir!) is to put this little book into your hands, and to desire you to *honour* the author in accepting, and to *divert* yourself in reading of it; for possibly, you may find so much *comedy* in this *walk*, as may dispose you to smile away an hour in the perusal of it. The relations are not *common* and *ordinary*, and perhaps as pleasant as they are *rare* and *unusual*. I do not know that any travel-ler, *jogging* in the *same* road, hath given the *same* account of things, or hath made the same descrip-tions which I here present you with; so that my remarks are *spick and span new*, and if they are *ridiculous*, they are not unlike the persons upon whom they are written. For the *Welsh* people are a pretty *odd* sort of mortals, and I hope I have given you a pretty *odd character* of them, and so I think I am pretty even with them for *oddness*. A *Taphy* is observed to be a trickish animal, that hath a vein of *Jackpuddinism* running through all his actions, and therefore I thought it not improper to sprinkle here and there somewhat of the *blue-jacket*, and to *Merry-Andrew* my progress a little farther as I went with jocund observations, that the *history* might be agreeable to the *matter* it treats of. So that if a *Welshman* is: a *jest*, as all the world ac-count him a living *pun*, a walking *conundrum*, and a breathing *witticism*; then have I made one joke upon another.

   I am not insensible that papers of another na-ture and complexion are more agreeable to the *character* you bear in the world; *Machiavel* and *Malvezzi*, or some discourse of maxims of *policy*, would be a more suitable subject for your Contemplation: But (Sir!) I pretend not to instruct you for the *Parliament-house*, but to divert you by the *fire-side.*

Now for the conclusion of all; if there are any *good things* in *Wales*, the enjoyment whereof is worth the wishing you, I pray Heaven to crown you with the fruition of them: But possibly it may be a province not much *crowded* with blessings; may you therefore flourish in the affluence of good *English* mercies; may you always possess good *English* riches, health and honours, and all other happinesses and prosperities of our own nation!

I am, (worthy Sir!)

Your very humble Servant,

The D—n Setting out on his Journey.

The Briton Described,
or a Journey Thro' Wales[1]

pon the first of *June*, having taken leave of my friends, and received a message, a little tiny errand to be uttered by word of mouth, together with a letter to be delivered into the hands of one of the most Reverend Taphies, I began to have some thoughts about *rigging* myself out for my intended voyage; and to that end,

---

1   James Bridge Davidson, in his *Conway in the Stereoscope* (London: Lovell Reeve, 1860), says (67) writes that this was not a work by Dean (Jonathan) Swift, as suggested in some editions, but of an inferior imitator. The latter would have sought to piggyback on the repulation of the more famous author to popularise the work. —Ed.

I spatterdash'd my legs with a pair of cuckold's boots, and either adorned or furnished my hand with a battooning cudgel; and having entertained in my retinue a whole *distich* of spaniels.

Upon the fourth of *June* I turned one side upon *London*, and the other towards *Wales*, the country which was to be the period and term of my journey. We travelled all that day with much pleasure, being treated, as we went, with the *delicacies* of nature: the air was *kind* and *soft*; the fields were *trim* and *neat*; the sun *benign* and *cherishing*: the whole creation was *obliging*; and, from every thing we met, we received a *civility*; so that this first day passed over with much satisfaction. I do not remember that we saw any thing remarkable, unless 'twas a fellow driving a *tired cow*, whose slow motion he now and then quickened by wringing the *pendulum* of her tail, and (as it were) curling it into a screw; he *twisted* her forward, and bored the air with this living *augre*; methought a very pretty trick, to make a wimble of his beast, and a handsome way to insinuate her along, and to improve her pace. 'Twas far beyond the courtship of a wisp of hay, in regard *fear* urges more than *flattery* can allure, and all creatures are more ready to ease their *backs*, than to fill their *bellies*: O how scorpions, pretty crabbedly applied, will make a thing caper, and increase his career far beyond the *temptation* of cake and marmalade! and a cat of *nine-tails* will drive better than a dish of sweet-meats can invite and draw. This was the method the bumpkin used to advance the *pro-*

gressive motion of the animal; which indeed is far different from the custom and practice of the *Creations*; for whereas this man made his beast proceed by thrusting at *one end*, the tail, they make their tir'd jades jog on by putting at the other, the *foretop*. We began to subscribe to *Cartesius*'s opinion, that animals were engines; for, 'tis like, the clockwork of the cow was somewhat disordered, and the machine (like a jack) was run down and stood fill, till this artist wound it up, and set the movements a going.

Being indifferently refreshed by the virtue of that passage, we went forward very couragiously, and, after a little time, were presented with the prospect of another scene, which was laid in a meadow by a river-side, where we overtook a *rat-catcher* and a *fisherman* disputing precedency, and the pre-eminency of their professions. The rat-catcher argued, that his calling was more worthy, in regard the object of his art was a *vocal creature*, whereas that of the fisherman's was dumb and *silent*; besides, rats are educated in courts and palaces, are more choicely bred, and have a more delicate diet than fish to feed on; plentiful reversions of roast and boiled, luxurious fragments, and the *magnificent ruins* of pudding and pasty, are their common dishes; only sometimes they pop on a piece of *bread* and *butter*, not of so wholesome a relish, that is, a little *arsenick* spread for them on the *trencher* of a chip; these are the *viands* of this domestick *vermin*; whereas worms and flies, and vile insects, and perhaps a hook to boot, are the best *fare* that is eaten by fishes. The fisherman replied, that fish themselves were food for men, but it was never known that rats were in season, unless in the *extremity* of a siege or famine.

We left these fellows very hot in controversy, which could not be decided, and passed on, till at length we arrived to a little knot, or *asterism* of houses standing, or rather lying, on the *crump* of a hill, raised somewhat *proudly* above the ordinary level; and, methought, looked down with somewhat of *disdain* upon the humble vallies. Who was the founder of this *hamlet* is not certainly known, but we perceived the *thacker* had been a great *benefactor*. As for the nativity of the place, the foundation was laid under an unfortunate *configuration* of the heavens; so that the *tinkers* and *coblers*, and the dregs of mankind that dwelt there, expected not prosperity, nor hoped to be advanced and sublimated into the *flower* of the people. The main *stress* of government lay upon the shoulder of a single man, who was a *bear-ward* by office, and, being the most substantial person, was thought fit to be *invested* with the sole authority of the township; a most proper magistrate for such wild savages! We observed that this village had as many ways *into* it, as it had ways out of it, which were equal in number to the points of the compass. The *purling* brook that crawled by it, the *recking* dunghill that breathed within it, the *crook-backed* elm that stands *cringing* near it, and the *pack-saddle* steeple that stood *squinting* over it, made a pretty draught of an handsome *landskip*.

The inhabitants of this place were much addicted to the vice of *stealing*; every things sticks to their pitchy fingers, and they have such an *attractive* virtue, that wherever they come, all things trot after the magnetism of their persons. A fellow squatting upon a cricket, in a room we were in, and rising up from his seat, the stool on a sudden (as if tack'd to his a—e) immediately marched after him, to the great amazement of the woman of the house, who did not suspect that his *bum* had *hands*, or that her *stool* so nimbly could have used it's *legs*. Another espying a *cylinder* of bag-pudding, pretty thick in the waist, lolling upon the table, whilst the hostess turned her back, in the very *twinkling* of her head, *pocuss'd* it into fob, and so shrowded it's dimensions into a second bag.

The *approaching* night, and our wearied *limbs*, compelled us to lodge among these tenements; having almost worn out ourselves by tedious travel, we resolved here to repair our *breeches*: but, alas! this *mending* (I allude to *taylorism*) was little better than meer *botching*. For, whereas we thought to have renewed nature, and to have recreated our palates with the pleasant wholesomeness of *rural delicacies*, we could scarce so much as even patch her up with the *burden accommodations* of a red-letticed inn; the *foretop* of a carrot, and a few parched pease, were our choicest provender, which filled our cavities so full of wind, that we thought we had got the *four quarters* in our bellies, which made such squibs of our breeches, that (like the fifth of *November*) we were continually discharging of *rockets* and *crackers*.

The next day dressed with *Aurora*, nay, before the had put on her *Indian* gown, we set out with the sun, who, bearing as company but a little while, withdrew into an apartment behind a cloud, at whose absence the heavens, *frowning* and contracting their brows, did presently fall a crying, and wept such plentiful showers of tears, that they moistened our skins with the *deluge* of their grief: but that which terrified us most of all, was *water*, which we saw of several colours, sometimes *red*, and sometimes black; which put us in mind of those prodigious rains the philosophers speak of, *blood* and *ink*; but, overtaking a *collier* and a *red-oker* man, we perceived 'twas the *distillations* of their budgets. But that which gave *wings* to time, and made it *fly* merrily while we were in the company of these vagrants, were the frequent *quarrels* that were broached between them, which, at length, were improved into severe *buffetings*. The *object* of both their occupations lies hid in the earth, and they work like moles, whose employ is *under-ground*, and (like a certain fish) they take their *colour* from the place they converse in. The collier thump'd, with *tincturing* fist, the red man black; and the red man dy'd with *vermilion* blow the black man red; so that we never saw before such a *party-coloured* combat, such a *fool's coated* conflict, wherein the stout champions were so mutually disguised, that they seemed to be *amphituos'd*, and to be wholly transformed into each other's person.

After another day's travel in dust and sun, we saluted a good handsome town, not a little resembling in crookedness a middle-sized *shoeing-horn*; at the entrance into it, the *uncarpetness*, as I may say, of the floor, or, in other words, the *unevenness* of the streets, somewhat dislocating the position of our almost *tripp'd-up* feet, had like to have demolished us, and to have thrown us down backward; but to prevent the *solecism* of kissing the place at the *wrong end*, we recovered our fall, and went bolt upright into the *navel* of the corporation, where there was such an *assembly* of provision as represented a market, which was unhappily disturbed by an unfortunate accident; for a *certain bull*, of an *uncertain* man, having mistaken his *box*, and taken *pepper* in the nose instead of *snuff*, and being enraged and heated by the virtue of the *spice*, took a risk about the cross, and emptied by his ramble all stalls and panniers; so that this *brisk customer* made a scrambling kind of dinner for the whole country, who were riding upon one another's backs for viands and booty, and were tumbling among the ruins of bakers, victuallers, and costermongers. We were informed that this town was much infested with the unwelcome visitants, *rats* and *mice*; insomuch that the inhabitants have a *rat-catcher* at a certain pension, as the only *talisman* against such noxious vermin.

Having left this town behind us, we came to a *wood* on our left-hand, nigh unto, which was a discontented fountain *murmuring* as it run (we did not enquire at what) and *bubbling* forth seemingly much dissatisfaction. This wood was a *promiscuous rabble* of all vegetables. A *throng* of trees of all ranks and qualities; we refreshed ourselves a little under this natural *arbor*, and being pretty chearful in this circumstance of place, one of our *caravan* began to express his joy in some notes of musick, who, as soon as he began to strike up with his *pipe* (thinking he had but one) he presently perceived it to be multiplied into an *organ*, and wondered (with the bumpkin that pulled at the bellows) that he had so much harmony in him. For you must know, hereabouts dwelt a thing called an *eccho*, who, as soon as the heard but *sol, fa*, whipp'd, the improved the melody into a *noise* and *concert*; and presently increased those single notes into the whole *gamut*; and most neatly played the *wag* with the *tail* of his voice; being a very pretty *songster*, that sings well by the ear. But while *lug* was solaced with the tattling *reverberation* of voice, our *eyes* were ravished with a most delicate prospect, for here was a most pleasant champaign piece of ground, which, extending and roaming itself some furlongs in length, was furnished with all the *excellency* that ever commended the most *transporting Elysium*;

the air was *lullaby'd*, as still and quiet as dormant infant; the day was orient, bright, and clear; the earth, like a forrester, was clad in green: the figure of this field was a *parallelogramum*, the stile was situate South-East by North, and consisted of a *climax* of three rails, over which we conveyed ourselves by *elevation of leg*; near the entrance into the meadow, we observed an hole or *casement* in the hedge, which we perceived the hogs had oftentimes *threaded*; but the hedger had *glaz'd* it with a *pane* of furz.

Having ambled over some furlongs on this, as it were, *Newmarket* heath, we perceived it to degenerate, and to grow worse and worse, and, like an handsome neck of mutton, to determine in the unevenness of a rock, or scrag. A little while after we winded a *cordwainer*, who (as, he told us) was newly recovered from a sad *mischance*; for, walking carelessly, one day he happened to have a fall, and to *squot* his breech upon an *hedge-hog*, which he carried away as cleverly (it clinging to his buttocks) as if he had sat upon a *ball* of his wax; whether there is a sympathy between a *shoemaker's* tail, and the skin of and *urchin*, or whether the *bristles* of the creature entered the *pores* of his backside, we list not to decide that controversy now; but, however, the more that *spinny* of awls had made a *cullender* of his a——e: but being not much concerned at the *cerebrosity* of his *sievy* bum, the *ilet-holes* whereof being not very deep, we went together, till we arrived to the *roughness* of the foremen-

9

tioned downs, which did somewhat decline into an uneven *precipice*, whose craggy stairs, as soon as we had descended, we stumbled upon an house, or a dunghill modelled into the shape of a cottage, whose outward surface was so all to-be-negro'd with such swarthy plaister, that it appeared not unlike a great blot of cow-turd: this structure straddled over about eight ells of ground,[2] above the surface whereof the eves were advanced about two yards, and the chimney peeped out about a foot above the eves; the light flowed in through the *old circumference* of a bottomless peck: which, being stuck in the thatch, supplied the place of an *orbicular* casement. The door-way was a breach in the wall towards one end, which being of a dwarfish size, *i.e.*, two foot lower in stature than an ordinary man, we were forced to abridge our dimensions, and to creep in. The parlour, hall, kitchen, *i.e.* one room within, was prettily adorned with the *poetry* of *ballads*; a *crippled* pipkin with a broken shin, near allied to a dish of the same matter; a vocal spoon with a whistle at the end; and a *tipsy* cradle reeling in the corner, methought, were a *pretty* fort of *goods*, and not *unhandsome furniture*. A whole *litter* of children was *strewed* upon the floor; only one *mop-beaded* boy was *tripos'd* on a cricket, and blew the fire; the carved mantle-tree seemed to be defended by a little *wooden* fellow, furiously strutting in an *oaken* cloak: and we perceived the window was *endorsed* with the picture

---

2   An ell is 45 inches in length, so 8 ells is 30 feet or 10 yards. —Ed.

of a fly. We observed that the *bulky* cupboard was a nusance to the whole *family* of houshold-stuff, which it had mightily disobliged by entrenching on their liberties, they grudging it so much room; and indeed the table, bed, and other utensils have not suffered a little detriment by it's injurious contiguity. We had a prospect of whole *territories* about this building, which, though not large, yet were exceedingly well fortified; a little hedge being a pallisado on one side, and a narrow trench, instead of a bulwark, on the other: the *continuity* of the mound was *violated* by a *notch* in the corner to set a stile in, over which, when we had passed, we espied a bank like a little *hybla*, capp'd with a hive of bees, which this small *Eden* curiously carv'd, and (as it were) *quincunx'd* into a knot, did feast with the moisture of it's delicious flowers. Leaving the *phylacteries* of this yard, we met the good housewife of this little tenement with her tippet *bristling*, her mouth *mumping*, and her hands *knitting*; she had a *cade* lamb at her *rear*, at tending upon her, and a *kitten* in the *van*, conducting her home.

We followed our noses from hence, and were directed by the *clue* of a long hedge; which, after a great extent in length, we found to be *tagged* with a rough lane; turning from which, a little toward the right, we overtook a *church* standing (like an ace) and moping by itself, at some distance from the town; which, whether it run from the parish, or the parish *from it*, we are not as yet informed, though we have most reason to suspect the *latter*;

in regard as to outward appearance, the weak constitution of the fabrick seemed not much to be addicted to run. It seemed to be very crazy, and had a *muffler* of ivy, which, we presume, were instead of crutches; for, whereas that feeble vegetable is usually upheld by the walls it clings to, we believe it was the *buttress* here to support the walls. But having saddened our aspect with the melancholy looks of this desolate temple, we took our leave of it, and shot directly down a *balk* upon that prophane town to which it seemed to stand related. At our first salutation whereof, we chanced to pop into a dapper *alehouse,* mightily stuffed with a huge hostess, whose moisture distilling through the pores of her body, and being somewhat turned through excessive heat, struck our *olfactive* nerves with so great a lowerness, that we had quite been overcome with this *vessel of vinegar,* had she not too much jogg'd herself by an unhappy fall, and spilt a great quantity of her unctious liquor.

The shoemaker conjectured that she had lost about five or fix pounds (*averdupois*) from her rear behind, and presently concluded, that she was in great danger of hanging all *a-one fide,* unless some charitable person should poize her with thrust of *assising nose.* We had scarce *primed* our pipes, but in comes a *law-jabber,* accompanied with the *bum-brusher,* or school master of the place, who, after some time, took occasion to shew their skill and breeding at fisty-cuffs, but (thanks to the stars) without any *danger* to their professions; for they did not so much aim at the *head*, as level their fury at each others heels, where their knowledge was supposed not to lie, though some hold that they have as much learning at one end, as they have at *the other*. The most remarkable thing in this village, was a carrot-pate house at the *posteriors* of the town; it was covered with tile, and was curiously contrived after the *Italian* models. The master that did animate, or the Ἐνζελεχία of this stone carcase (they told us) was lately dead: his distemper was a *quarrel* between his belly and his back; the one being *bursten* took pet and run away from the other, so that the poor man, being at a loss for a place to put his victuals in, *dy'd* with a conceit.

St *Crispin*'s disciple, having a mistress in this lordship, and being almost within the *atmosphere* of her presence, began to *wind* her, and had a great tendency to the place where she was; so that I might as soon expect that a stone should fall beyond the center, as that this *gentle craftsman* should budge further; wherefore nothing was expected now, but an immediate *divorce* from each other's company; but before we parted, he obliged me with the prospect both of her person and fortune. As for the first, as soon as I saw it, I had greater reason to congratulate my eyesight than I had before; for she was blessed with a most *ravishing* aspect, and a snug face, most prodigiously graced with a dainty fine nose fastened in it's middle; which is not like some snouts that look more upon one cheek, than they do upon the other, but shews equal respect to both, not at all *disobliging* the right by *steering* too much on the left. And then for her eyes, they are excellent at twiring, and will be sure to keep her nose *safe* (I'll warrant you) for one looks one way, and the other *another*. The woman had a mouth too, which was somewhat bigger than that of a musket, though not twice as big as the capacious bore of the blue noggin. This mouth she put but to *one use*, and that's the same that we put ours to, that is, to eat three our four meals in a day; for it seems, whereas other women often use theirs in *prating* and *twattling*, we perceived that this *saved* her *mouth*, and spake through her *nose*. As we have given you the picture of her person, so now let's present you with a landskip of her fortune. As for her lands, that is, pasture-ground and meadow, we could not discern, but that (like a spot upon the globe) they took but little room upon the surface of the earth, and (like the possessions of *Alcibiades*) were but a little speck to the world. A little muck would dung her fallow; one high table t—— (to speak in the *Oxford* dialect) will much enrich it, and an ear of corn will go near to sow it; 'tis like she hath grass enough for a couple of rabbets. Having surveyed the paramour, and the portion of this nivelling cobler, after a single sip of fixes out of a tin pot, and a *treble* go-down out of a cup of *double*; after a *right line* scrape with *left* leg, and uncouth doffing of a bad bonnet, after *slinking* a compliment by way of thanks for his society, attended by his *coblerhood* to the confines of a yard, at the clasping together of two lowering gates in the presence of a *corpulent* and *burly* elm, I solemnly took leave of my fellow traveller. After his departure, I was forced to beguile away the time in the shady *solitude* of silent thoughts, which before I spent in the *brisker entertainment* of discourse and dialogue: I had not long busied my faculties with inward speculations, but I met with variety of objects courting with their *flatteries*, my almost distracted contemplations. I saw *three stones* so artificially set, that they represented the figure of a convenient *stile*. Methought the architecture of it was very curious; for one stone, about a foot square, being placed perpendicularly upright, it's northern extremity was crossed by another at right angles; on the other side whereof, was erected another perpendicular correspondent to the former. The position of these materials made a pretty fabrick, over which a man might commodiously pass; it's surface was smooth, not *tufted* with snags, which are always catching and *snarling* at your cloaths, to the great *disguise* and damage of your breeches; about two yards distance there was a cross delved in the earth, which seemed either an argument of *Popish superstition*, or a sign or mark of the parish *selvidge*.

Departing from hence, we moved through a close very *populous* with mutton; there being (as it were) a whole *academy* of sheep *seizing* on a hay-rick, not bottled out into commons, but geometrically carved into good *sexangular* luncheons. 'Twas foot-cloathed (as it were) with straw near five yards about, upon which were tumbling a *bag-piper*, and an *hocus*, who wantoned so long till (like dogs) at last their play determined in a sharp conflict. The man of musick buffeted the juggler to *some tune*; who adding two or three *howls* to the *notes* of his drone-pipe, by cleanly conveyance, did vanish from him. The piper appeared of a tawny complexion, his *nose* bending with an arch upward; his *eyes*, being somewhat hollow, seemed to increase the *promontory* of his jetting forehead. In a word, there was *charm* enough in his aspect; he was well built, his whole *frame* and contexture was *sweet* and *regular*; I must needs say, I have seldom met with any handsomer *model* or *platform* of a man. But though his *person* was neat and *uniform*, yet his habit and *garb* was full of *deformity*, and there were as many *solecisms* and *incoherencies* on these, as there were *congruities* and beauty commendable in that. He wore a *miscellany* of apparel, a *gallimafry* of cloaths; as I humbly conceive, it was a *tythe suit*, composed of various and several sorts; such a *club* of rags, and *rendezvous* of fragments, must needs be a collection (like the jerkin of the jay) of several feathers from divers birds. His doublet (which indeed was but one great patch in *folio*) was very *heterogenous* from the rest of his attire; he had worn his lappets into perfect *fringe* (so that he seemed to be surrounded with the *remnant* of a curtain) and had *thinn'd* his elbows into their first *principles*. It was of a mouse-colour hue, and (as near as I could guess) it appeared to be the *result* of an old cloak; both it's first *crop* and *latter-math* too were both worn off, and it was so thread-bare that it had almost *foundered* three or four of his best lice; wherefore we advised him to hang it no longer on a *knave's* back, but to condemn it to the housewifery of a shoe-clout. The relicks that were left of his tatter'd breeches, were one *story* pendulous below his coat. His instrument (like a gizzard) was tucked under his arm, which, by *shog* of elbow, he did *hug* into harmony, and *squeeze* out of it's womb most ravishing ditties. We made but few remarks on the person of the juggler, only we thought it appeared to be somewhat *sleathy*; his noddle was shrowded under the *patronage* of a colloped hat, whose *indented* margin, being somewhat frail, declined from the equality of an *horizontal* position, and flapping inward on both sides, and hugging his ears, forced the poor man to look as it were through a *spout*. He had a bunch of rib-band in his hand, which possibly might be the effect of his last *vomit*; for we suppose, having had a surfeit of silk-worms, and a *loom* in his *throat*, he can *disgorge* more at a cast, than an ordinary weaver can work in a week's time. His little *pointing-stick* and tin dishes, with other implements of his art, made an horrible noise and *combustion* in his pocket, even to the terror and amazement of an *humble-bee*, who was rioting on the luxuries, and was wantonly *basking* on the funny *terrace* of a magnificent thistle. Nay, the jingling of his tackle did alarm an army of *wasps* and *hornets,* which lay *encamped* hard by under the roof of a lady furz-bush; these made such an onset on hocus with their *landsprizades,* that making a *pin-cushion* of his body, they stuck it so full of needles, that the *pungency* of their weapons and *artillery,* piercing to the quick, made the poor fellow curvet and elevate himself nimbly into two or three dancing *capreols.* He carried on his back as thick a *quickset* of stings, as a hog of bristles. He was swelled to a treble proportion beyond what he was; his *hands* were grown too big for his pockets, and could have no reception into those narrow *closets.* The *circumference* of his head was hugely increased beyond the *diameter* of his hat; so that the *convexity* of the former, could not be contained within the *concavity* of the latter. In a word, being magnified beyond the *fallacy* of the best glass, his cloaths were too little for his *enlarged* dimensions; so that he burst thro' the confines of his *scanty* case. Means presently were used for levelling of this mountainous vagrant and hideswol'n; he was immediately plunged into a bath of honey, which, though a present cure of his disease and malady, yet was as great a cause of an inconvenience as bad; for a certain *bear,* not far off, got his medicine in the wind, and came galloping, for a lick of her admired dainties; which, when the juggler perceived, having lost, through fear, the retentive faculty, he adulterated her dish by a mixture of somewhat that was of the same colour, though not so sweet. The juggler *hoofed* it away with a winged speed; the bear, with a pair up and a pair down, most swiftly pursued him. We staid not to see the issue of the race, but advanced forward in regular progressive motion, who, after a little time, were crossed by a rivulet, which wriggled along with a crooked current; over which we conveyed ourselves by *saltation*. On the other side of the bank was a little *Arabia* of sand, enough (I suppose) to supply all the *hourglasses* in the country: nay, perhaps, and that of *time* too till the last minute: near this mountain of sand, lay prostrate at length *two iron-wedges* contiguous to a block in *folio*, which we supposed was to be rent into collops, and to become a *sacrifice* to hungry *Vulcan*. There was a numerous *family* of chips about it, which were different in shape, colour, and bigness, so that they seemed not to be the offspring of the same parent; they lay in a *chaos* without any order; amidst which confusion, the unlucky *Gibeonite* that hewed them, lost the head of his ax: the *decollation* whereof seemed ominous to the man, and made him superstitiously leave his work: myself, and a couple of *Gadarens*, that were driving swine, made a diligent scrutiny for the *noddle* of the tool, which, after some time, we perceived to lie entombed under the *mausoleum* of a good lusty shaving. We did not perceive that it was much damnified by it's retirement, only the dampness of it's *urn* did somewhat abate and obscure the eagerness of it's edge, and the lustre of it's aspect. We delivered it into the hands of it's owner, who presently fastened it to the shoulders to which it did belong.

After a small offering of thanks for our careful search, the swine-herds turned to the left, and we wheeling to the right, after we had jogged over some few acres of a *phlegmatick* and cold constitution, most happily popped on the *warmer* turf of a pleasant corn-field. It was *fringed* about with a mound: of elder-trees, whose ambitious height and luxuriant branches gave impregnable security to the nestling birds. The *diameter* of a path run through the midst, whose *poles* were transverse, or thwarted the hinges of the world. It was environ'd on both sides with a *sea* of corn, which being moved by the breath of *Æolus* (that bellows of the world) what a *flux* and *reflux* was there of *waves* of wheat! We passed through this territory and dominion of *Ceres*, with the most exalted delight. How did that *Goddess* fit in triumph there? What crowds of *clients* bowing their ears to her commands and dictates? Every land was parted with the *isthmus* of a balk, on several of which lay the *habiliments* of the harvesters; an extended sleeve of a red waistcoat, embracing the collar of a leathern jump, and touching the hem of a grafted petticoat, presented us with the idea of a pretty *wardrobe*. We went out of this inclosure through the western passage of a *three-railed* gate: upon which there did directly shoot the *aged* fragments of a *decrepid* wall;

which over-topping our stature in height and tall-
ness, we were forced to add to our quantity, a nine
inch stone, that, raising our dimensions, we might
peep over it. There was scarce any thing, remark-
able on the other side, unless a vast rolling-pin of
human ordure. It was four inches diameter, and,
probably, discharged from a *musquet* bore, and
that near upon the confines of a turf of wormwood,
whose bitter scent, mixed with the unsavouriness
of *excrementitious* atoms, breathed a medley kind
of stink, and gave but ordinary entertainment to
our offended nostrils. Among the ruins of this
mound, we discovered the snout and some other
limbs of a *murthered* dial; it was not so defaced,
but that we could discover in it's *physiognony*
some *martyred* figures, that were yet legible, and
there were some relicks of lines that were not quite
obliterated. Time, I presume (being vexed per-
haps that it should observe it's motions) hath set
it's grinders in it, and out of envy and malice hath
quite devoured it. I am apt to think that this pile
of stones stood in its native country, where it was
first bred, as, may be conjectured from an adjacent
pillar, whose pregnancy (we fancy) produced this
litter of stones, it being the mother of these *rocky
babes*. We advanced to the orifice of this lapideous
womb, where were hewing mortals, by cruel *mid-
wifry*, digging out the offspring of teeming earth.
It was an *unpolished* spectacle, and the workmen
were as *rough* and *uneven* as the prospect; and the
artificers were as intractable and stubborn, as the

materials or objects of their art. Two of the most *brawny* paviours food lolling by the mattock that picked them out, and a single one, in a decumbent posture, lay prostrate at their feet, whose northern extremity performed the office of a *pedestal* to the *embryo* of a statue, which was but newly hatched, and fashioned in a bed of sand. The declivity of a corner, near the entrance into the pit, gave occasion to the water to *stagnate* into a puddle; through which we did not fail, though the trajection was very short, but fetching a circuit about it's shore, we went out at the passage through which we entered. But no sooner had we conveyed ourselves out of this *hole*, but, after we had traced over some few furlongs of a *grassy pavement*, a certain moiety of our bodies popped into *another*, and a few steps after, of our feet happened into a third; and, a little while after, falling down, our hands were buried in two more. We wondered who had punched so many eyelet-holes in the earth's skin, till seeing *Robin Run-a-hole* fit mumping (like a Troglodite) in his house under ground, we perceived the inclosure we were in, was a well peopled *warren*: we had a frisk or two after the inhabitants of the place; but their *heels* prevented our design on their *scuts*, for the nimbleness of the *one* secured them from imposition of *salt* on the *other*. The *sanctuary* of their burrows, defended them from the violence of all *persecutions*. Their *cells* were contiguous, nay, in some places, they had broken down the partitions, and, by a frequent *burglary*, did invade the privacy of each others apartments. The *dragon* that kept this *garden* of conies, was a *Zamzummin* in stature, a second *Goliah*, whose hand was quarterstaffed with a mighty beam. They told us of an *Hercules* or two, that came to encounter this keeper, who ('tis said) did so *out-club* the yermin, that, instead of an *auger-hole*, he made them earth themselves in the asylum of a *coney-hole*. The *burrow* of the keeper stood near the centre of his dominions, being the *metropolitan* seat of that little nation of rabbets. The *architecture* of the fabrick was not contemptible, being stately in height, whose top was crowned with the magnificence of *turrets*, whose vigilant loftiness had an eye to the security of the circumjacent region. The biggest wonderment we beheld about it, was, that it's *head* did not shoot so far *upward* into one element, but it's *feet* sunk as low *downward* into another, it standing knee-deep, nay, almost up to the waist in earth, having as many stores under ground as it had above. Whether the bucks or does were the *pioneers* that dug those cellars, or whether the architect designed them on purpose to prevent the under minings of those notable *delvers*, we are not so well able to determine. We espied in a corner, a *wooden stratagem* or two on purpose to entrap, (we supposed) ensnaring reynard, so that that living *gin*, so fatal to pullen, died himself in a *wile*, and one *trap* was *trapann'd* by another. It was a well-contrived *ambush*, and pretty handsomely victualled with a good lusty *temptation*, which so wrought upon reynard, that he could not, by any means, resist it's charms, though it is thought he was as wise a fox as any in *Æsop*, whom we never met with, without a piece of *mortality* tacked to their tails.

Having passed the bounds of this *rabbet-limbo*, it was not long before we were embraced within the confines of a spot of ground like an orchard; for the ranges of vegetables gave us a shrewd suspicion that *Pomona* had had her residence in that place. Here *Autumnus* stood lolling under the pressure of a burden, being scarce, able to bear so many *wreaths* of fruit. His head was crowned so, that it bowed with apples; so that shaking his ears, as we passed through, he did so pelt us with a *shower*, that the unlading of his *noddle* made *fractures* in our pates, and raised *tumours* in *sinciput* as big as *Kentish* pipping. The place was pretty *populous* with trees, the *squadrons* whereof seemed to be well disciplined, standing in their ranks, and as it were in *battle-array*, like a well ordered army. Here were several degrees of vegetables in wonderful subordination-one under another, from the *commonality* of shrubs, to the *majesty* of a cedar. Here were inferior and *superior*, and (as it were) *dignified* fruit-trees; among whom there stood a pear-tree, I suppose lord *primate* of the *hierarchy*. In a South-west corner we espied a few *vermiculating* hops, wriggling like worms up the *pyramid* of a pole; near which stood an elm-tree in the *arms* of ivy, which hugged it so close, that it was almost *incorporated* into it by it's *clasping* embraces. The *posteriors* of the elm-tree were most barbarously *chastised* by the prickles of a bramble, which the *breath* of *Æolus* would often move with smart jerks. One of our company taking an occasion to pass by one of these unseen briars, they presently had their *talons* clawing upon his back, and frighted the man as much as the bush did *Demosthenes*, which, catching him by the coat, made him (supposing it to be an enemy) to cry out for quarter: but the fellow being *cased* in leather, and the *buffness* of his coat being armour-proof against the bristles, and as it were *hedghogism* of their prickles, they could not fasten their fangs in his garment, wherefore (thanks to his stars) the man had no hurt, but was blessed with a great de-liverance. Toward the bottom of this orchard lay prostrate the trunk of a slain *myrtle,* and that not far from the verge or shadow of a *cops* of beans, pretty tall in stature, and well branched; by the *coverlets* we saw there should be beds not far off; I suppose they were the *lodgings* of carrots, turnips, and of other roots. There were *cabbages* grown to a commendable *globosity,* the roundness whereof tempted us to a game at *foot-ball*; we banded them aboat sufficiently, and made some of them caper over a ten foot wall. One of the gamesters was hit just in the mouth, the bore whereof, being too little for the bullet, could not receive it into it's *orifice*; but, however, it *gelded* and damped it's fury, so that it did not retort with violence to the injury and detriment of any body else. We had sweat longer at the recreation and *Olympick* sport of *kick-cabbage*, had not the breath of *Cloacina* (her habitation being near) been so strong, and was a nusance unto us.

So that being struck out of our *quarters*, we turn'd our *quarters* upon the *stink*, and travelled over a grate into a church-yard: the track of our path lay between the mansion-house of the *Levite* on the left hand, and the *church* on the right; behind which, towards the South, there *stood*, or *lay* (we cannot tell which) a weather-beaten tomb, which was *mouse-eaten* at one end by that vermin time, that nibbles all things: it seemed to be an inverted *hog-trough* turned topsy-turvey, with it's muzzle downward; but whether it was or not, or whether it was purposely erected as a *monument* to preserve the memory of those; ashes that lay under it, we cannot tell, though we have some reason to suspect the former, in regard there were so many swine a digging about, who, with the natural *spades* of their noses, had almost made a *pit-hole* for the *stone*, and so had like to have buried one *grave*, in another. Here was a whole herd of swine a rooting, as if they had been turned in on purpose to root up *Christians*, as they are in the fields in *Italy* to dig up turfles. A little *wall* lay sculking about this territory of the dead, which we supposed was placed there as a *bulwark* to their ashes, but it proved but a feeble fence against the intrusion of the lambs, who made frequent *capreols* into this adjacent dormitory. The mound was raised a little, and capp'd with turf, and environ'd with the hollowness of a good handsome ditch; but yet neither cap not ditch could keep these animals from *leap-frogging* over them, from grazing in a *charnel-house*, and from turning a *cæmetry* of shades and ghosts into a *feeding pasture* of hungry beasts.

We mounted this wall, and moved on towards the western period of our intended journey. The bordering close was, *pimpled* with mole-hills, which seemed but young *protuberances* not blister'd into the bigness of some neighbouring banks. Leaving this ground behind us, we descended the declivity of an adjoining pasture pretty well *bearded* or *bristled* with thorns and bushes; and so passed through a farmer's yard, where we saw an *Alps* of straw, with swine (instead of snow) a groveling a top on't; which put us in mind of the *ambition* of goats, who are always clambering up the crags of rocks. The western extremity of the wheat-hovil shot directly up the barn, an *appendix* to which stood the *apartment* of the hogs, over which was perched a roost for poultry.

Not far from this country *Tusculum* stood the *island* of a house in the embraces of a moat, like *Tycho*'s *Uranoberg* in the midst of the sea; an ancient pile, a reverend *nest* of as venerable a *bird*, which having taken her flight hath left it a solitude. The greatest observables were a little silent *bell* in *duodecimo*, which, being utterly *disteepled*, hung between the collops of an old wall, or rather a *mor-*

tar inversed, which had lost it's pestle, so that it was not vocal by stroke of *internal clapper*, but by knocks and blows of *external hammer*. Within the sound of this bell stood a lolling *washing-block*, being a wooden kind of anvil, where the *She-Vulcans* were *hammering* out, with battle-door, the filth of linnen, whole unctuous distillations were the *Nile* that watered the little *Egypt* of the adjacent garden

Having moved from this mansion about three or four furlongs, we passed by the skirts of a *rotatile* engine, in shape not unlike an house, being *pack'd-salt* at top with a ridge: it seemed to stand upon stilts, and to be a moving habitation like those of the Gates. 'Twas *prefaced* with a *portico*, into which we ascended by a scale of stairs. The whittling wind breached a *vertigo* in it's pate, whose giddiness, communicating a motion to it's grinders, made it *whirlegig* the grain into flour. A little distant from hence, beyond a small sandy desart, stood a village, whose *steeple* was in it's center, not unlike the *mast* of a ship. This tower, as to outward appearance, had a *portly person*: yet they told us it had the imperfection of dumbness, it having been *disbell'd* for some years. They were alarmed to church by the report of a *musquet*, which the clerk (being an eminent *gunner*) did usually discharge at every man's door. This clerk was a *weaver* by trade, and had relation to a *loom*, wherein he had been *ambling* for several years with one foot up, and the other *down*, and, with all his treading, had scarce got cloth enough to repair the breaches of his tatter'd elbows. They told us that his trade and he had lately been at *cuffs*, and are just upon parting, it being such a *limb-wagging* profession, that he is not able to endure the *penance* of it. This man had a wonderful skill in *sweeping* the church, and, it is thought, could tell what a *clock* 'twas at the *South*, dial as well as most *astronomers*; he was also a pretty man of *his hands* for *singing*; for when the tune one *Sunday* had ambled from him into the chancel, and had almost caught a fall among the *non-songsters*, really they told us that this *notable* man gave it such a neat jerk, as that he *twitched* it into the church strangely. Now, I say, for the clerk to have a rare knack of securing the hymn from those that would steal it, oh! 'tis an excellent thing! The most remarkable things in this town were an *ecclesiastical* wall made of *secular* mud, which mounded in the introduction of the parsonage: it afforded secure harbour to *vagrant bees*, who, rendezvousing here, became a *colony*; they made so many cells in it, that it appeared to be the fragment of a reverend *honey-comb*. Not far from this grew a tree in *folio*, an huge, thick, squot elm, *pounded* within the circumferences of four benches, which we supposed to be seats made on purpose for the *posterns* of spectators, when *Whit-sun-ale* is solemnized with *festivity* of fiddle, and celebrated with *caper* after pipe and tabor.

Immediately after our departure from this place, night overtook us, whose *sables*, eclipsing the splendor of the day, shortened our course, and *crookened* our career aside to look for a lodging. An happy *retrospect* obliged us with the *prospect* of *glimmering* thatch, which, the nearer we approached, the more visibly it appeared in the shape of an *house*. It was called, by way of irony, a *castle*, whose governor was a decayed *taylor*, who having lost, through an *unfortunate* hole of his pockets, his needles and thimbles, those *chattels* of his breeches, and implements of his vocation, was reduced to poverty. The man was *nimble of foot*, though a *dwarf* in *bulk*, so that nine of such might very well club to the *elementing* of a man. After a small collation of *tripe* and *buttermilk*, we tripp'd up a ladder to the apartments of our several cabbins, where, with the *poppies* of sleep, we refreshed our noddles, to the great comfort and satisfaction of our wearied carcasses. After valediction to pricklouse,[3] the next morning we set out with the sun, and had not went above a mile or two, but we heard the rumour of a sad *disaster* which had lately befallen a country Corydon, which was the loss of a whole pound of candles, supposed to be stolen by some *highway* rat at one *robbery*. The relations were various as to the manner of the theft; some say he carried them away behind him, like a *burden* of sticks; others say, that he hung them by his side like *bandileers*; but most agree, that he laid them upon his shoulder one by one, and ran armed away with the luminaries as with so

---

3   (*derogatory, archaic*) A taylor. —Ed.

many musquets. We were somewhat amazed at the horror of that sad story, fearing left we ourselves should be a prey to those bold *banditti*, who, being pretty *greasy*, seemed to be a good handsome *bait*, and lo, being mistaken for *rats-bane*, might be *pouch'd* by the vermin: but (thanks to the stars) we escaped the fate of the bishop of *Mentz*, and marched on upon the *forehead* of a smooth mountain, upon the summity whereof *squotted* another hill; but it bore no proportion to the seat it fat on, being but a *pimple* to it, as that was but a *molebill* to the whole globe; it put us in mind of *Pælion* clambering upon the back of *Offa*, that false heraldry of the giants hill upon hill, by which bunches they thought to have scaled heaven; the *crown* of the uppermost was somewhat depressed and sunk into the *hollowness* of a little valley, about which stood the natural *bannisters* of some thorn bushes, whose folding branches weaved into a *lettice*, which, *threaded* by the sun-beams, *dappled* the ground with a pleasant chequer-work, and yielded besides a good handsome shade to the panting sheep, whose fleeces discovered them to have taken sanctuary here against the *persecutions* of the violent heat; for the cattle feeding within the covert, and rushing through the brake, every briar took *toll* of their coats, and *excis'd* their backs, as fast as they filled their bellies; on every sprig there hung a fragment of their *liveries*, and the whole hedge was *cloath'd* with tatter'd fleeces, as if wool had been *vegetable*, and had grown there. These *spoils* were looked upon as excellent booty to vagrant youth, who went about stripping, plundering, and, as it were, *sheep shearing* the hedges: we met a crew of these *pickering* wool gatherers, the very *emblems* of beggary, and but once removed from the vilest *rascality*; one shoe a piece, and half a hat, a *remnant* of a doublet, and a *moiety* of a sleeve, a pair of *dispocket* breeches, and a jagged jump, were the flower of their accoutrements, except two or three locks of wool, tuck'd like scuts under their girdles, as a *badge* of their profession; and some cramm'd stockings *bobbing* at their sides, as *trophies* of their pyracies.

Some few furlongs from hence there was a mixt *assembly* of kine and goats at dinner upon the *lawns*; their meal was interrupted by the unwelcome salutes of troublesome breezes, whose *stimulation* of rump did engender such a frolick, that, with *curled* tail and toss'd-up horn, they run gadding and bellowing, and with their vocal frisking, with a pleasant kind of terror, did at once both *recreate* and affright the astonished beholders: the magistrate or *herdsman*, that kept these animals, was in the midst of the tumult, who, finding himself miserably involved in a *hubbub*, with furious club chastized their gamesomeness, and with mighty bustling becalmed the uproar. This fellow was a strange creature, wonderfully *goth'd*, and *all-to-be-vandalled*, even to barbarity itself. A clown in grain! an uncultivated boar! a beast of the herd in human shape! We proposed a query or two about the *genius* of the place; he told us the soil was cold and big with clay, and would doubtless yield a good *harvest* of tobacco-pipes; and as for the people, he said they were a *pan pudding* sort of people, much addicted to that vile sort of creature. A whole table at a christening is spread with a *yard* of *pudding* and a *balk* of beef, a *ridge* of one and a *furrow* of the other, which did so wonderfully work upon their chops, and made their mouths so water, that two of the chieftest *grandees* of the town, the *hogherd* and the *heyward*, fell seriously to snouting for some few morsels; the *two-ear'd* pitcher that stood upon the bench was Mr *Prinn'd* in the scuffle, *i.e.* lost a lug in the fray; and we were informed afterward, that the *distaff* lost a lock or two of it's flaxen *perriwig*.

Among *rational* wonders, the most remarkable miracle of this place was an eminent *cotquean*, a *meer* woman in the habit of a man, a kind of a *malcut-purs'd* creature, an *epicæne* animal of a *twisted* gender, who hath a *petticoat* soul in a *trunk-breech'd* body, and scandalizeth virility by skill in *housewifery*. He spins (they say) like a spider, and makes his wheel giddy by a swift *vertigo*; we observed him to be *stately* in his gate when he advanceth up to spindle; and, indeed, was *retrograde* again with no little gravity. He is a learned *craftsman* in the making of diet, a notable *food-framer*, who buffets the cream till he hath *frighted* it into a consistence, and knock'd it into butter, and afterwards squeezes with dexterity of sift. He was endowed with the gift of toffing of pancakes, and had a wonderful knack at tampering the materials of a bag-pudding. He surpassed the dairy-maids in *milk-pan* accomplishments, and was excellently qualified for a meal-tub office. He squeezed the curds with *cheese-press* bum, and kneads the dough with fulch of elbow. He is a *critick* at sweeping, and manageth the beesom with mighty skill. We could hardly discern any mote of dust, he having *dislodged* from crevice even the smallest atoms; we were dazzled with the *sun-shine* of his radiant *brass*, which was exceedingly enlightened by *modern* cleansing, he being a singular scowerer, and very knowing and able at sand and *oistershell*.

This *hen-housewife* mortal lived a monkish kind of life, being cloister'd up in a desolate habitation of a certain gentleman, who, we suppose, does see him to dwell there to affright the mice, and to be a *bull-beggar* to the rats; and also to terrify a worse kind of *vermin*, which we call *thieves*, who are apt to creep through the *mouse-hole* of a window, and to nibble away the furniture of a dispossessed house; or possibly he might abide there to repair it's breaches, and to recover it from it's craziness, and, by the wholesome *physick* of frequent fires, to keep it in *health*, and to persuade it not to tumble, but to remain still a mansion to the family that owns it.

We tasted here of the hospitality of this fæ-masculine wight, who spread a joint-stool with several sorts of viands; which, though not very *delicate*, yet the variety might atone and make amends for their *meanness*. Here was the *epidermis* of a hog, the outward skin, called the *sword* of bacon, which was infected with the jaundice, and looked yellow; here was the hull of a peasecod plundered of it's pease, and corned with salt, some broken fragments of sheeps trotters St *Lawrenc'd* on a gridiron; the offal of a lark, the minced spors of a *bootless* cock, a skimm'd quadrant of soft cheese, well sauced with the *butt ends* of forked scallions, the mouldy reversion of an *antiquated* loaf, dipped in the verdure of water-cresse pottage, afforded us the refreshment of a pretty collation. By the virtue whereof, being somewhat recruited, we moved forward and crept up the *brisket* of a small mountain, upon whose sloping descent stood a quadrangular *sheep-pen*, which we passed through, and found pitched with *buttons*, a pretty sort of floor and modern *Mosaick*. Not far from the most eastern hurdle (as near as we could observe) leaned a ruinous bridge, which gloried in the passage but of one arch, and that seemed rather natural than *artificial*; for the impetuosity of the cur rent, having bored an hole through an heap of stones, licked it into the shape of an indifferent arch; at the foot whereof stood a smith's shop, about a bay of watling; it seemed to be a pretty reverend seat, as we gathered from the mantle of green moss upon it's back; though it was covered with stubble *without*, yet it was pretty tolerably furnished with iron *within*, as thread-bare horse-shoes, bits of keys, some few semicircles of iron rings, odd links of *interrupted* fetters, and a broken series of a discontinued chain. The *Vulcan* was in his den, and was hammering out hobnails for country hoof. His forge was raised from the ground like an *altar*, upon which there did burn, as it were, a *vestal* fire, which blast of bellows made much to bubble up in this little *mongibel*. What cinders were belched from this flaming *Vesuvius*, whose smoak and ashes besmutted the *Pluto* in this infernal region, who having primitive apparel, *i.e.* being *skinn'd* over with a case of *leather*, and having a swarthy complexion, did, with the *grimness* of his aspect, and with the horrible *rustle* of his breeches, fright one of the dogs of our company into a fit of sickness; we imagined the cur might mistake him for a *tinker*, who is commonly a *disease*, or at least a *nusance*, to those creatures.

We saw nothing hereabouts very remarkable, only we met several mastiffs laden with the *cargo* lusty bones in their mouths; they were ambling east ward; a very fine spectacle to see a regiment of curs trooping along, instead of *Bilboa*, armed with *shoulder-blades*. We wonder'd at first from whence such plenty of *anatomy* as to furnish them, till spying the carcase of a dead palfry, we perceived they had been feasted with the viands of his flesh, and stole the skeleton piece-meal. A baker chanced to come by through a gap near at hand, mounted upon just such another *morsel*, ripe for collar-maker, which, being surprized with the spectacle of his brother *carrion*, took an occasion to start, and to disburden himself of his load; which sad misfortune proved a lucky accident to the dogs, whereby they were furnished with *bread* to their meat.

Not far from hence was a scurvy slough, most fatal as is observed, to Millers, whom it sups up into the *abyss* of it's profundity; we saw one moving *a-tit-up*, *a-tit-up*, till he Bounced in, and, by a most disastrous *pitch-pole* into mud and dirt, discoloured his coat, that was candied with the *effluviums* of his meally bags. The *necklace* of bells about the crest of his beast ceased to be sonorous, being quite choaked. His meal, through fright and moisture, was metamorphosed into pudding; and spunging up the liquor, it grew so heavy, that it *thrived* into such unweildiness, as that it was almost unmoveable: we cautiously waved the danger of this dirt by diverting a little toward the northern parts of this quagmire, and so in a dainty fine path, and that not meanly beautified with variety of flowers, we continued our journey very prosperously, only one of our company had a most calamitous fall over an unhappy clod of the *first magnitude*, which, undermining his pedestals, gave him a preposterous *squob*, his head saluting the ground first, to the great detriment of the *outward man*. There run parallel with this path a pitched causey (as we supposed) about ten furlongs; we stepped into it, and followed its track till it brought us into the desart of a common, not so much as accommodated with horse, tree, house or man, so that here we felt the rigour of somewhat called hardship, the stomach barking, the hoof galling, the winds whistling, and the heavens dropping; all these conspired to make us miserable. At last arriving to the borders of the wilderness, we were courteously received into an hospitable hamlet, where we enjoyed the blessing of an indifferent refreshment. We took up our quarters here that night, and passed away the evening in some pertinent queries about observables in the place. They presented us with a *pretty curiosity*, which seldom occurs, and that was the copy of a brief, containing the losses of a distressed virgin, which, because the form and stile is somewhat unusual, we care not much if we here insert.

The Copy of a BRIEF

To all ladies, gentlewomen; whether maids, wives, or widows, or others of that softer sex, of what state and condition soever; whether waiting-women, sempstresses, spinsters, bawds, punks, doxies, and all other petticoaters, from those who through *wantonness* have naked *backs*, to those who through want have naked bums, greeting.

W*hereas we are credibly informed by our trusty and well-beloved* Roger Thwickwack, *of* B. *in the county of Salop, jumper, and* Arthur Twitchbox, *smoaker,* Cadwallader Whipwhop, *wrestler,* Anthony Snug, *fidler,* Giles Firker, *bumbrusher, and several others of the like laudable* professions, *That our beloved subject, Mrs* A.

C. *of the town and county aforesaid, damsel, hath lately sustained a great loss by a most lamentable misfortune, which on the fifth of this instant most miserably befel her after this manner following:*

There was a certain glass-case of a gad-fly *colour, i.e. a little inclining to a calf-dung yellow, and somewhat of a dwarfish size, not much exceeding the stature of a cricket; it was supported by the strength of a double thong, at the* North-west *point of her chamber, where, for some time, it had continued in a* pendulous *posture, and had arrived to a great repute of* civility *and meekness, whereby it did much exceed, and frequently put to the blush, the other utensils of her chamber.*

Now, this poor thing, by reason of the rudeness of two lusty pusses, *whether affrighted at their* caterwawling, *or it being not able to bear them in the* acts of love, *we cannot tell; but certain it is, it let go it's hold, and, after a dismal manner, came blundering down, attended with the ruin and desolation of several* jiggumbobs, *and jimcracks, to the great lo and detriment of our poor distressed subject.—The particulars whereof are as follow:*

1. *The ivory* gums *of a* toothless *comb.*
2. *A little* bottle-breeched *glass, replenished with* love powder.
3. *A brace of* blind *needles, that lost their* eyes *in the tumble.*
4. *A* double *scut of an hare tied up with a* single *pack-thread.*
5. *The* latter end *of an old broomstaff.*
6. *The* butt-end *of an old sugar-loaf.*

7. *The true-lovers* knot *made in wire.*
8. *A square bit of tip.*
9. *The margin of a broad bar.*
10. *One finger-fall.*
11. *Two tags.*
12. *A crack'd glass with a club-foot.*
13. *The skin of an onion stuffed with arsenick.*
14. *One whisker of a bearded arrow.—The loss of which tackle and implements amounting to a sum of great value, we do send our letters patents to beg the charitable benevolence of all well-disposed persons, hoping that they will be pleased to take the* deplorable *condition of our unhappy subject into their* serious *considera-tion:—For is it not a sad thing to lose so com-modious a place to lay pretty things in, and all by the misdemeanour of two* unmannerly *cats? For where will this our subject lay her* gal-ly-pots *and syrups, her gums and pomatum? Had these* mouse-hunters *only eased nature there, and then gingerly departed, they had been very excusable; but first, to come slily into a lady's chamber, and then to* squobble *and fall out there, and, in the midst of their quarrel, to pursue one another to the top of a shelf, and there to renew the battle again, and to box one another till themselves did fall, and to demol-ish that very thing which supported them in their bickering; as the* fool in the fable, *saw'd off the bough he sat on. Oh! this is a sad thing.*

Another *living observable*, we met with here, was the fragment of a physician, whose pretenc-es to learning were very great, but by converse we found him to have more *stomach* than *brains*, and therefore was like to have more consolation in a *kitchen*, than in a study; for there, perhaps, he may find a *jobb* of work for his *grinders*; whereas he knows not what to do with his books, unless he should act the moth, and eat them. One of our company perceived his parts to lie more towards the *powdering-tub*, than his *pharmacopæia*; for whilst he is busy in the *former* he may keep himself *alive*, but when he reads in the *latter*, he kills his patients. We had some roast-beef to supper, and we commonly found him within an inch of the dripping-pan, with an *acre* of bread in his hand, which he call'd a sop, with which, when our backs were turn'd, he usually spung'd up the dripping, and cheated sir-loin, and robb'd it's knighthood of it's due moisture. A scholar of our company perceived him to be well read in papers, that skreen the back of a limb of roast, and that he found a great deal of matter in the socks, that are on the soals of minc'd-pies.

I shall here present you with a copy of a *Welsh* surgeon's bill.

Dr Davy Shones, *a* Welsh *Surgeon, his bill at* Ofwestrey, *for* Mrs Suesanna Madox.

Sept. 9, 1730

	l.	*s.*	*p.*
For dresing hur mortify'd elcere upon hur lege, and clen it from stinkin, with spirits of chamfire, tinct, myrhe, an udder dings praper for 49 tims. 15 tims it cost me 2 *s.* 6 *d.* evry tim, before I cowd get the stinking flesse away, and the oder 34 tims	3	1	6
For lancin and scallin the boune	0	10	0
For ungts. ols, and linimt. to anointe the stinkin lege	0	7	6
For pills aurea guilded with goulde	0	7	6
For drams and cordiolls for hur and hur companeons	0	7	6
For lodgen, care, and attendunce upon hur	1	12	6
For running away, and hindrin me to have tim to make hur cure to perficteon	2	10	0
For envy, hatred, and mallis, and ill-will in spaaking, uttrin, and purnouncin sevrall reflecshons, and fuls stores up pon me and my hous	1	12	0
For brekin my glas in the glas windows, with hur hors is nos	0	1	0
£	10	9	6

After a day's journey from hence, we set our feet

upon *Welsh* turf, and indeed were strangely sur-
prised at the *uncouthness* of many things that did
salute us here.

The country is tuck'd in on all sides with the sea,
except on the east, on which part it was *ditched* in
from *England*, by that *notable delver* king *Offa*,
king of the *Mercians*: over this dike if any *Welsh
man* chance to skip with his sword by his side, by
king *Harold*'s law, he was to lose a *branch* of his
body, *i.e.* his right arm was lopped off by the king's
officers.

Some think it had it's name from it's *godfather
Idwallo*, son to *Cadwallader*; who, with a small
crew of *Britons*, at the arrival of the *Saxons*, hid
themselves in this corner. Others suppose them
to be the *spawn* of the *Gauls*, from whom they
seem to be but a few Aps removed; Ap *Galloys*, Ap
Gauls, Ap *Wallois*, Ap *Wales*.

As for the *inhabitants*, they are a pretty sort of
creatures, which, when we saw, we were so far from
stroaking them with the *palms* of love, that we were
almost ready to buffet them with the *fist* of *indig-
nation*. They are a *rude* people, and want much
instruction: for, when we consider the *soil* from
whence they *sprang*, and the desarts and moun-
tains wherein they *wander*, we cannot but think
that greater pains should be taken in cultivating
and manuring, in discipling and taming them, in re-
gard it is harder for a *bearward* to teach civility to
the *beasts* of *Africa*, than to those that come from a
more *mannerly* country:—We do not say, when they

are in their country, they do (like bears and foxes) live in woods and forests (for, I presume, they have more *sun* than *shade*, and so more fire than *wood*) but if we agree with *geographers*, and are of an opinion that they are inhabitants of a *wilderness*, and are *landlords* of a common, as I and every-body else are owners of the air, we must beg their pardon for our conceit. We have been informed, that they were dug from a *quarry*, and that they dwell in a *stony* land, so that if we compare this kingdom to a *man*, (as some do *Italy* to a man's *leg*) they inhabit the very *testicles* of the nation. And, I pray, what are those but the vilest of creatures, that breed as well in the privities of the *greater British* world, as those that are hatch'd in the *pudenda* of the lesser? But whether *Welshmen* are the *aborigines* of their country, as crab-lice are the *autocthones* of theirs, and proceed only, like them, from the *excrements* of their foil, we shall not here dispute. They are of a *boorish* behaviour, of a *savage* physiognomy; the *shabbiness* of their bodies, and the *baoticalness* of their souls, and that, which cannot any otherwise be express'd, the *Welshness* of both, will fright a man as fast from them, as the *oddness* of their persons invites one to behold them. Some of them are such *rude* and *indigested* lumps, so far from being *men*, that they can scarce be advanced into *living* creatures; nay, they are such unmanageable *materials*, that they can scarce be hewn into the shape of *blocks*; much labour and art is required therefore to make them *statues*.

They are not so much given to *fighting*, as by a speech, it appears that was utter'd by hur nown countryman, who, when drawn out upon some design, began to pur and murmur after this manner:

> Hur hath worn out hur freez *preeches*, and all hur cloaths; and now hur can get no money to keep hur, or to buy hur some *cows-baby*, and hur could hear nothing but *marsh, marsh!* and drums beat, hur was therefore, once for all, now resolved to fight no longer, but to go into hur nown country.

—They are much inclined to *choler*; for hur *Welsh* plood is soon mov'd, and then hur *stamp* and *stare* and scrat hur pole, and vent hur fury in *uds-plutter-a nails*, and will fight for hur life in battle at fisty-cuffs.

The whole nation (like a German family) is of one *quality*; for as every lord's son is a *lord here*, so everyone is crown'd with the title of *gentleman there*; so that hur country is a good *pasture* for an *herald* to bite in, who can't chuse but grow-fat among such worshipful *genealogies*. We were much surprized at the thoughts of their rank, and did not suspect so much gentility among such a people; when we saw so many *coats* without *arms*, we could not imagine they had any with them, but fancy'd they had more need of a *taylor* than of *Clarentius*, and of a pricklouse to stitch up, and compose their *breeches*, rather than an *herald* to blazen their *families*. They appear'd to us to be very ill accoutered gentry: but, however, vileness of *equipage* is no blot in *escutcheon*; as may be easily made out from this following narrative: when king James commanded all that were *gentlemen* in an army, to pass by him, he, observing a *rag-a-muffin* to hobble in the rear of the train, commanded him to be stopp'd, because he looked not like a gentleman; but *Taphy*, cry'd out, that hur was as good a shentle man as the best, only hur cattle was not so good. In their *travels*, they care not much that their horses should drink with a *toast*; as appears by the wrath which *Shenkin* discovered, whom his quaffing beast had *pitch pol'd* into a river. *Uds-plutter a-nails*, (quoth he) in a great fury, what, cannot hur trink without a *toast?* He took it much in dudgeon, that the jade should be so *bold* as to make a *sop* of his master.

They do not always observe the rules of *justice* in their punishment; oftentimes chastising one body for another, and so *misplace* their rigour on the undeserving, as will be very evident from this following instance: A certain *taylor*, ferrying over a river in their country, with a *diminutive* nag; the steed never using to travel by water, and wondering that he *stood* still, and *mov'd*, was possess'd with fear, and made some *disturbance* in the boat, to the great endangering of the passengers: the *Welshman*, being in jeopardy, was *fir'd* with anger, and, without any wings, he *flew* on the Taylor, and revenged the injury of the *palfrey* on poor pricklouse. The *stitcher* swaddled the *scrupling* horse, and *Taphy* beat the *stitcher*, to the great *diversion* and grief of the spectators.

The *materials* of his apparel are usually a well shagged *freez*, so that we cannot call it *sleepy*, being fleec'd with a nap like any sheep-skin: it affords excellent *harbour* to the vermin of his body, which, whether it be stock'd with store of *joicements* of them, he commonly signifies by the *symbol* of a shrug.

His *fashion* is generally a pair of *oblong* trowzers made of a brace of cloak-bags, suppos'd to be twins; these, tack'd together, are a perfect *emblem* of his *crural* attire. This garment had *conjugal* affinity to a thing call'd a doublet of the same lineage; a copious vestment, very roomthy and capacious, able to comprehend both his arms, in the single pudding-bag of one sleeve; it's uppermost *confines* were hemm'd with the scanty *dimensions* of a contracted collar, but it's lower *extremity* was bordered with the *paraphrase* of amplified lappets. The *summity* of his head is commonly crown'd with a *Monmouth* cap, and it's *crown* is commonly *pinnacled* with the *battlement* of a button. Cuffs are an *innovation*, things which their ancestors were seldom guilty of; and, indeed, bands and clean linnen, are an *upstart* invention; being the modern effects of pride of their huge ones, whereas *primitive britishment* was never acquainted with the *habiliment* of a *shirt*. Their feet, it seems, are of an hot complexion, for they often air their *distockin'd* pettitoes; and if they had any hosen, they were the *offspring* of their drawers, to which they were fasten'd by leathern *ligaments*. The *perfection* of a *Welshman's* equipage, the *cream* (as it were), of his accoutrements, and that which compleats even his most *festival* attire, is (as the story goes) an old sword of hur nown breeding, which hur hath brought up from a tagger: and this he can brandish, with much valour, against the tremendous on-set of *dragooning* bees; a kind of enemy which the *Taphy* is much afraid of, in regard he is always arm'd with a pike in's rear, which, once upon a time, being fasten'd in his forehead, *broach'd* such a pore in his *physiognomy*, that he could never endure those *hum-buzzing* shentlemen (as he calls them) in yellow doublets.

The country is mountainous, and yields pretty handsome *clambering* for goats, and hath variety of precipice to *break* one's neck; which a man may sooner do than *fill* his belly, the soil being barren, and an excellent place to breed a famine in. It is reported of Campania, that it was the most noble region in the world, the air *pleasant*, the soil *fertile*, the *theatre* of *Bacchus* and *Ceres*, where they were at *fisty-cuffs*, for the preheminence; but we perceived no such *scuffle* in *Wales*; for those deities are so far from *fighting* there, that we could not discern that they were so much as ever there; there being scarce water and oatmeal to give us *being*, we could not expect *Egypt* and the *Canaries*, butts and granaries, to give us a *well-being*: there is no *Canaan* to be found in the arms of a *desart*.

The *commodities* of the nation are chiefly wool-
len cloaths, as cottons, bays, &c. of which their tat-
ter'd backs are an ill sign of; for sure they are not
so silly to furnish *other* countries with raiment,
and to go naked *themselves.*

As for the *diet* of the *Briton*, it is not very delicate,
neither is he curious in it; for if he should, his *appe-
tite* perhaps might curse his *nicety*, and by pleasing
his *palate*, he may starve his *belly.* A good mess of
flummery, a pair of eggs he rejoices at as a feast,
especially if he may close his stomach with *toasted*
cheese; a morsel of which he hath a great kindness
for. You may see him pictur'd sometimes with that
crevice in his head, call'd a mouth, charg'd at both
corners, with a *crescent* of cheese, and himself a
cock-horse on a red-herring, and his hat adorned
with a plume of leeks: good edible *equipage!* which,
when hunger pinches, he makes bold to nibble; he
first eats his cheese and his leeks together, and for
second course, he devours his horse. He never much
car'd for a *sop*, since, once upon a time, it *drank* up
all his drink, and would not club to pay his shot.

As for his *person*, his stature is of the lowest
fize, not above a stair or two above one *story*; and
we found always a cock-loft, and that usually *emp-
ty.* His face usually *bubbles* into tumours and pus-
tles. Besides the natural *haut-goust* of body that
breathes from grain, he usually sends forth an
artificial smell, which you may wind as far as the
extreme *unction* of twenty funerals, only the *scent*
is not so sweet: he smells as rankly of the *single*

stink of brimstone, as a gold-finder of a *medly*; for a scurvy disease, commonly call'd the *scrubado*, makes frequentlyan in *road* into his person, and invades his body; so that he is forc'd to choak his enemy by stink of sulphur. 'Tis a *creeping* distemper, whose progress is check'd by mortification; so that when he *leaves off* his shirt, that is, when it *leaves* him, and can hang on no longer, it is excellent furniture for tinder-box, as *virtually* containing in it both match and tinder.

The *musick* he plays upon is a tool stil'd an *harp*, that is, a *triangular* stick *bed corded* with variety of extended catlings, which he *tickles* with as much dexterity, as if prentice to *Amphion*, and draws as many *boys* after him, as he did *stones*; nay, *these* we have seen in some places to trot after him; but not so much to *admire*, as to *pelt* him for his harmony. He puts his instrument to one use more than the ancients did theirs, *i.e.* he *purveys* with it for maintenance; so that when sustenance fails him, he strikes up for a morsel, and so lives by *sounds*, and (*camæleon* like) hath *alimony* from air. He *serenades victuals* in every village, as the *pied-piper* did *rats* at *Hamel*, and he allures *luncheons* after him, as much as the other did *vermin*: here a knob of bacon wags after him for *one* strain, and there a *crust* follows him as a reward of *another*; one hits *him* in the mouth with a payment of *pottage*, another *pops* him in the *pocket* with the *gratuity* of a *carrot*; he is laden sometimes with such plenty of *beveridge*, that he can't jog for his fraught; all which variety of *fragments* is the most ample *income* and wonderful *revenue* of his skill in musick. His usual admirers are country milk-maids, whom vibration of string doth move and stir into jig and measure; and whom *breeze* of *instrument* (like those in *tail*) do chafe and tickle into dance and caper: by the *wagging* of his noddle, and the *wriggling* of his limbs, he seems to be taken with the *accents*, or else to be bitten with the *tarantula* of his own musick, which hath *infected* him into a galliard, and caus'd him to fig about with a frolick motion.

We could not perceive that they were guilty of much *learning*, of which the *lowest* degree is several *notches* above their most exalted capacity. We met with one pretty *proband* in the alphabet; but, for the most part, the knowledge of the least *iota* is rare and unusual. A man skill'd in *orthography* is admir'd as a *sophy*, and a writer of his name is term'd a *rabbi*. The *top-gallant* of the parish possibly may be so wise in *hieroglyphick*, as to scrawl the character of a *mystick* mark, though such deep literature is not frequent amongst them. Some of their ancestry have *smelt rank* of Astrology; one whereof, *Merlin* by name, was very *notable* at the stars, and most intimate with the planets; insomuch that sometimes he would *fling* at a futurity, and venture at a prognostick concerning the weather. 'Tis supposed he was bred up at the feet of some *She-Gamaliel*, being so well vers'd in the prophecies of old womens corns, and who could as cleverly foretel rain, as the learned *almanack* of the most weather-wise toe.—The study of *wizardism* hath also been famous amongst them; one goodman *Druis* was well accomplish'd in that kind of learning; hence formerly a *wizard* was stil'd a drue. This fellow (they tell us) was the *schoolmaster* of *Pythagoras*, into whose *breech*, 'tis said, he in fus'd, by birch, the opinion of *transmigration*. He was *dextrous* at a fortune, and *old-dog* at augury; the only thing we dislike in him, is, he sacrificed men, and so divin'd by *butchery*.

To the *wisdom* and *philosophy* of this sophy, his little boy *Bardus* added *poetry*; a lad, it seems, notably inspir'd with *flames* and firebrands, with heats and raptures, and such kind of *tackle* that are us'd by poets. The disciples of this *laureat* were term'd *bards*, the great *embalmers* of heroick actions; who, I warrant you, will wrap up an atchievement so securely in a *monument* of a single verse, that all the nibblings in the world shall never be able to devour the *immortality* of a name. They *ballad-sung* the praises of renowned heroes, and, in lofty strains, *wire-draw'd* their fame, and *stretch'd* their glory to after-ages. They were in huge *esteem*, and had the *cap* and *knee* of the greatest commanders, insomuch, that if two armies were even at *cuffs*, or at *cudgels*, and a venerable bard had stepp'd in but with one *foot* of his poetry, they would have held their *hands*, and have thrown down their *hilts*, and have hearken'd to the advice of his learned *dactyles*, and l not offer to snout it till his *poetical* worship had been out of danger. The most famous of these *metre-mongers* were *Robin Plenidius*, my gaffer *Glaskiron*, and of late years old farmer *Davy*, and our neighbour *David ap Williams*.

The *champions* of the country, men of celebrated prowess, were Mr *Cassibellane* and Sir *Nennius*, Knight, the former whereof was so doubty a blade, that 'tis said he confronted *Cæsar*, and bid him kiss his back-side with undaunted *gallantry*; the other, grappling with the same emperor, did *diswhiniard* his hand by main strength, and sent the man home laden, with some stripes, and with a *naked* belt. A notable, instance of *Welsh* valour! To these may add that, *Hector* of *Britain*, the renowned *Arviragus*, who was so great a raw-head and *bloody bones* to the *Roman* soldiery, that 'tis thought he frighted them, even to the *bewraying* of their breeches, and made them mightily *stink* of a *filthy* discomfiture.

As for the *loves* of Britons, the intrigues of their *amours* are not a little remarkable; they being very pretty *animals*, when *disguis'd* with that passion: they are *tinder* to such flames, being quickly set on fire, even by the least spark, which, when it hath catched the *match* of their souls, (for they have *brimstone* in them, as well as in their bodies) they are presently kindled into *transport* and *ecstasy*; and these model them into the shapes of a thousand *anticks*, and make them shew more tricks than *Banks*'s horse. Sometimes they are shaking the *globules* of their noddles, and sometimes dancing some geometry, with the *figures* of their *feet*; now they smite with *clapper* of fist their troubled breasts, and anon found out some knells of dismal groans, being variously affected according as the *weather* is in their *Clorinda*'s face; if *aspect* be clear, than is Taphy *serene*; if brow be cloudy, then is *Morgan show'ry*. He commonly o'er flows in his prattle, about the *princum prancumness* of his mistress, and is witty, even to a jest, on the fineries of her habiliments, in describing of which is pretty lucky at *similitudes*, and is happy in his *comparisons* about her person. One, having a glympse through the key-hole of her *saffron* body, burst out into a pangyrick of the *bees-waxness*, as he phras'd it, of her tawny complexion; and seeing her *tippet* to bristle into the erectness of a *turbant*, he fell a laughing at the *coxcomb*, as he term'd it, of her coif and head-gear. He seldom troubles his madam with the salutation of a letter, but usually accosts her with the *missive*, as I may say, of his nown person, which being broken up in her presence, *out-fly* the contents full of fame and rapture.

Shentle modest! when hur see,
The fair looks hur made at me,
Hur could not choose by what's above,
But be entangled by hur love.
Hur was not think it fit and meet,
To wrap hur love within a sheet;

But was think it great deal better,
To speak her louse, than write a letter;
Hoping hur not exception take
At hur for hur country's sake.
What if hur *Welshman* be? What then?
Taffies was all shentlemen;
Born from *Venus*, that fair *coddess*,
And many other *shentle* bodies;
Part humane and part difine,
We are descended from *Jove*'s line.
All this truth hur dare not mince,
Being the issue of a *British* prince.
If should with *Shenkin* drink some wine,
Hur would not think hur fortune fine,
And hur would tell such tale in ear,
That all the world was never hear.
The shentle modest let hur prove,
Honest *Shenkin* will hur love;
Though hur was very filthy fit,
That drives poor *Welshman* out of wit;
And if hur will not pity hurpain,
Hur will never loufe again.

We heard of one that went a wooing, with a gun upon his shoulder, being resolv'd, it seems, if love be a *warfare*, not to enter unarm'd into the camp of *Venus*; still as his coy *Daphne* shifted from his presence, he march'd *musqueteering* about the room, and most fiercely pursued her, till, at last, in the brisk encounter of a close embrace, this warlike instrument took an occasion, somewhat unmannerly, to go off, and blunderbuss'd the mistress on her *breech*, on one side of the house, and poor Taphy on his *nose*, on the other; so that; being much dismay'd at this unhappy accident, one scrabbled one way, and the other another, to the total separation of a pair of lovers, and to the utter spilling of a *mess* of love.

They are pretty devout in their worship, though the exercise of *religion* is somewhat scarce, and have a pretty *glowing* zeal, though their churches are *few*, and at a great *distance*. 'Tis almost incredible how far they are fain to trudge for a little *homily*, which, when they have expected, have been *mump'd* with a *sermon* ten times worse; for, on such *raw-bone* livings, there cannot be expected very *plump* parts. The ordinary revenue of a spiritual preferment, may possibly be about *five marks per annum*; a bay of watling for a dwelling, endow'd with no more glebe, than just what it stands upon; only, perhaps, it may be *howe-stall'd*, with as much ground as may hold a *fly* for the pig, and a *roost* for the pullen. These divine cottages are usually situated some leagues from the temple; so that the holy man; with crab-tree truncheon, sets out with the sun, and stretcheth his *legs*, with a good handsome walk, before he arrives to *pulpit* to stretch his *lungs*, and wears out much of his *soals*, before he can reach his *stall* to mend their *souls*. Their houses of prayer are generally *thatched tabernacles*, which being steeped, as it were, with a *louver-hole*, seemed to be really that what the *temple* resembled when prophaned by the *Jews*, I mean, rather the pictures of pigeon-houses, than holy *sanctuaries*. They are wainscoted towards the East, with little desks, like pounds, where Levite, imprison'd for about half an hour, *fodders* the poor Taphies with some melancholy *tear-fetching* story, about a grim fellow called *death*, who *ambles* folks on his back into another world; a thing which he heard from the oracular gums of his *edentulous* old grannum, as she sat in the settle in the chimney-corner. Some of the most reverend rectors are dignified with a stipend of *six pounds* a year, besides the *perquisites* of a drum and fiddle; which, well managed on a holyday, make up a very pretty thing. Others have an *augmentation* of a bull or a bear, which, being solemnly baited about twice in a quarter, do pick pretty comfortable tythe from the spectators pockets, and make the poor parson's purse to smile and *mantle*.

Their *recreations* are various, but not much different from those in *England*; you may see them some times smite a *ball* at the rebound, and to send it on errand to their antagonists, which, being retorted by way of answer, is *rejoindered* back again with much dexterity. They will bandy to and fro this *missile globule*, and *shittle-cock* it to each other with great celerity. Their lungs are pretty good at a bubble in the air, which *meteor*, arising from the womb of a walnut-shell, they will make *fly* through the *welkin* on the wings of their breaths, and for a considerable time, by the blasts of their mouths, will support the being of those *emblems* of mortality.

In the *whity-brown* evening, or in the twilight, they run hobbling about their common, with *kites* at their heels, certain comets of paper, which they tow along with a tall string, and make themselves merry with the length of their tails, which are a large *series* of jagged toffels, tagg'd with a candle, as with the twinkling of a star, Happy is the man among them that can most discreetly manage this artificial planet; and he is presently *dubb'd* the very *Phaëton* of their country, that can most swift-ly career it with this little *lanthorn'd* Phæbus. The *scrubs* want candle on *earth*, and yet they must needs be sticking up *lights* in the socket of *heav-en*; there is scarce half a pound in a lordship, ei-ther to scare away darkness, or to *work by*, and yet these rascals, forsooth, will be *studding* the sky with luminaries to *play by*.—As for true and real *hunting*, there is no such thing among them; only they have, as it were, the *picture*, and some kind of *resemblance* of that pastime; for, their principality affording them but few hares, they course a *lock of hay* in lieu thereof, and alloo the *puss* of a good nimble wisp. The *whim* of it is this; when they have a mind to refresh themselves with somewhat that is a-kin to, or with an *idea* of, hunting, they make diligent search for a furlong or two of smooth and champaign ground, which, at last being found, they purchase a bundle of the swiftest hay (if *Irish* it is the better, for there are the best runners of all forts) this they expose to the fans of *Æolus*, which, being presently started by force of puff, it scuds away, and the dogs pursue it with mighty speed. In rainy weather they have also their *in-door* divertisements as well as other nations, such as *rump-pressing, hot-cockles, chap-smutting, snap-apple*, and the like. Some are cunning at the *cock-hall*, not so much for *picking* off the meat (though they are good at that too) as at throwing it with accuracy, and *chequering* the sport with *variety* of tumble.

As far as we could perceive, they love *holiday* fingers, and care, not much for encumbering them with that *inconvenience* called *work*. They can, shepherd like, loll upon a crook pretty handsomely in the field, and can discharge a *superintendency* over the goats. They are most accomplish'd *drovers*; to which laudable function they are so naturally prone, that they are apt to *drive* sometimes *more* than their own.

They are much addicted to the sin of *nastiness*, wallowing in filthiness like so many swine; so that the whole province seems to be but a general *sty*. You may swear they are made of earth without a metaphor; appearing like so many *dirt-images*, or like that of *Prometheus*, made of clay. The meaner sort of women are generally such *draggle-tails*, that the cattle in their bosoms are *quag-mir'd* in the filth of their *well gleeb'd* attire; so that the frisking fleas are so far from *Levalto's*, that we are verily persuaded they can scarce pull out *proboscis* and their feet from the bogs.

The *tenements* they live in are suitable to the *guests* that possess them; for as these seem to be *dirt* moulded into *men*, so those are the same matter kneaded into *houses*; they are usually very *humble* cottages, and low in stature, so that a man may ride upon the ridge, and yet have his legs hang in the dirt; those that are so magnificent as to be *crested* with a chimney, are mightily valued, as most *cocking* fabricks. We were not so vain as to expect very splendid furniture in such contemptible *huts*; but we soon perceived what utensils were most necessary; a dishclout and a beesom, and such cleansing *implements* are very proper to correct the filthiness of their mansions; we found no apartments in these their habitations, every edifice being a *Noah's ark*, where a *promiscuous* family, a *miscellaneous* heap of all kind of creatures did converse together in one room; the pigs and the pullen, and other brates either trackling under, or lying at, the bed's feet of the little more refin'd, yet their *brother* animals. The country is fortified in some places with a pretty *sprinkling* of castles, which, whether they naturally grew out of the rocks, or were artificially *ingrafted* there, may be a matter of dispute; some fancy'd them to be *stone-pits shot* up into the air, which represent the figure of vast buildings.

Wales is the most monstrous *limb* in the whole *body* of Geography, for it is generally reported to be without a *middle*, or, if it hath a *navel*, it is yet a *terra incognita*; for we never could find that ever

any man dwell'd there, the natives confessing them-
selves to be only *borderers*. Surely the reason why
they do so much affect the *circumference* of their
country, and abominate the *center*, is because they
are ashamed of the dominion; and, indeed, it is a
sign they have but a little kindness for their nation,
who, like unnatural sons, run from their mother,
their country, and, when out of her embraces, never
return again. A *Welshman*, when once abroad, hath
no more tendency *home*, than a stone an inclination
to fall up ward: he will trot over the globe, and rath-
er endure the infliction of any exile, than the cruel
punishment of being *banish'd* home; if he is once
on this side Dee, neither *hunger* nor *husks*, nor any
kind of hard ship shall drive him on the other.

We could not, in our travels, wind very many
feasts among them, the shabbiness of their soil be-
ing not able to nourish and pamper luxury; so that
a cook, unless he exercise on himself, and dress his
own fingers, is immediately starved here for want
of employment. They make some little invitations
perhaps to a *kid's-head* or so, and will junket with
hop-tops, with brisk alacrity. Such plain, mean,
and, as I may say, *borough* food, was even their
festival entertainments; but as for any *embroi-
der'd*, and, as it were, *metropolitan* mess, such as
bisks and oglio's, we never so much as heard of
them in their territories.

Their mart for law is a parish town, call'd *Lud-
low*, where there is a court of judicature, *deck'd*
with a judge, counsellors, attornies, sollicitors,

and other *furniture* which *embellish* the law: hither they trudge for decision of case, and here *redcoat integrity* dispenses *equity*. Most of their indictments are generally the tragical effects of some dismal *counterscuffle*, where a bloody *nose*, and a broken *shin*, is ample matter for the commencement of a suit; for, they being of a fiery temper, sometimes choler is kindled by an *antiperistasis* with a pot of ale; and then they fall to biting and scratching as hard as they can drive, and the wounds of this *caterwauling* and bickering afford stuff for an action the next day; which, being once got into the *pounces* of a *Welsh* attorney, is *dandled* into a business of no small aggravation. Oh! how these pettifoggers will hug a buffeting, and improve a squobble! They are the very *bellows* of contention, and will soon blow a *spark* into a great *combustion*. They are a kind of *tinkers* in the law, who usually *make* holes on purpose, that they may *mend* them; nay, sometimes they will play at *loggerheads* themselves, to set others together by the *ears*, and so (as if fighting was contagious) will *infect* the Taphies into quarrels and blows. One marching along the streets, advanced the *scolding* of two women into an huge *tumult*, as duels swell into great wars; and made the *snarling* of two dogs *thrive* into an action, and the fighting of mastiffs to end in the court of *Common-Pleas*. They commonly broach quarrels, and incense the shentlemen into knockings and smitings; crack'd crowns and black eyes, into assaults and batteries, and all for hopes of a livelihood that may be *skimmed* from the benefit of such wars: but perhaps the *spoils* from the skirmishes of such *clients*, are as rare as *pillage* from a *Scotch* army. The usual crime for which they stand generally convicted, is that great transgression and *sin* of *mice*, the nimming of cheese, and the filching of oatmeal, and of the rest of the good creatures that are arked in the cupboard; and, as they *offend like* vermin, so are ordinarily *taken* so; too, that is, not *apprehended* like men, but *entrapped* like rats; after which they are convented before the sage *puss* of the law, which, purring upon a tribunal, together with his *kitling* officers, doth fasten on the prey, and doth so suck and claw it, till it hath mumbled out all it's *blood*, that is, all the *money* of it's veins, and then wholly devours it. This, I say, is *one* of their offences, though not the *only* one; for some of them have been lash'd for an attempt upon *hen-roosts*, and have received condign punishment, even for stealing of poultry at the *wrong end*; for *Taphy*, it seems, having filched a chicken by the breech, did *disrump* her by his theft; and therefore, in resemblance to his crime, was almost *disrump'd* by punishment; so that, for stealing the *bird's* tail, he had well-nigh loft his *own*: a pretty circumstance observed in their justice and a laudable way of proceeding according to *lex talionis*.

For several crimes they have various punishments. That grand enormity of *breaking wind* is chastized there as it is in *England*, that is, the hand of magistracy doth usually inflict a pretty lusty *cobbling*, that is, for every report the loss of an hair, though some that have been much addicted to that infirmity, and therefore have been very *guilty* of a stink, have endured the cruelty of tormenting fairies, that is, have been pinch'd into manners, and a better *smell*. Artificers, when at work, punish any unhandsome action, by a particular severity peculiar to themselves, which they call *pursing*. The execution whereof is after this manner: The malefactor being prostrate on a block, two of the same occupation pull, as *discreetly* as they can, his drawers as close to buttock as a Spaniard's breeches, so as not to be laid hold on by the most curious pincers; the *pavement* of posteriors being levell'd and smooth'd from any wrinkles, a third artisan strikes it with a rule, whose smart application, by *quick jerk*s, makes some impression of pain, and so moves the blood as to raise and start a tincture, and (as it were) the *flea-biting* of a blush. Some of the more obstinate criminals are punish'd by *suspension*, but not by the neck, as here in *England*, but by the wrists, *thumb-rop'd* together with a string of hay, and so fasten'd to a peg; well! this is but the beginning (and as it were) the *hissing* of the punishment; do but mark, and the *sting* will follow: the offending Taphy thus dangling in the air, the beadle approaches with a stick *imp'd* with a feather at one end, and tickles his testicles; these softer titillations engender some *vibrations* of body, and nimble friskings, which are shrewdly chastis'd by a surly *cat-of-nine-tails*.

The cattle we saw most *legible* on their mountains, were goats and heifers, a runtish sort of animals, of a *dwarfish* size, but very *hardy*, of a flinty constitution, *calculated* on purpose for the *meridian* of a rock, on which (it seems) they can as heartily feed, as an *ostrich* on an anvil. Great numbers of these are often *disembogu'd* into adjacent countries, which, after some time, *circulate* home again in a *stream* of money; which yields wonderful refreshment to the fainting dominion, almost sick for the comfort of such a cordial. We perceiv'd their herds to be frequently mingled with little palfries, a stunted fort of horses, diminutive brutes, *shavals* in short-hand. They are *lower* in stature than an *ass*, but much *swifter* in foot, and very strong; as it appears from their burdens, which are oftentimes the *fortune* and substance of a whole family; for when a mortal breaks, he mounts all he hath on a *Welsh nag*, and travels under the character of a *Scotch pedlar*. We chanc'd to see a team of this small cattle, a rare spectacle, being (as we suppos'd) the least that ever was heard of, unless that which was harness'd in *Venus*'s chariot, which was a team of doves. These *British* steeds are so brisk and mercurial, that the people would persuade us, that a *Taphy* on a *tit*, would outstrip in travel an *Arabian* on a *dromodary*; a thing almost incredible, though the *pricking* up their ears, and the *stricking* up their tails, is an argument of their mettle, and may give some colour and ground for the assertion.

That which we admir'd most of all amongst them, was the *virginity* of their language, not de-flower'd by the mixture of any other dialect: the purity of *Latin* was debauch'd by the *Vandals*, and was *hunn'd* into corruption by that barbarous people; but the sincerity of the *British* remains *inviolable* tongue (it seems) not made for every mouth; as appears by an instance of one in our company, who, having got a *Welsh polysyllable* into his throat, was almost choak'd with *consonants*, had we not, by clapping him on the back, made him *disgorge* a guttural or two, and so fav'd him. They usually *liquify* the most rugged mutes, and soften 'em by pronunciation; melting the word tug into tudge, as is clear from this distich:

> Still did he *tudge* hur ear
> In praise of the *tirteen* seer.

i.e. did tug hur souses with elogiums of hur country. Whether the *Welsh* tongue be a *splinter* of that universal one that was shatter'd at Babel, we have some reason to doubt, in regard 'tis unlike the dialects that were *crumbled* there; however, whether it be kin or no to other country speeches, it matters not; but this we assur'd of, it is *near* and *dear* to the folk that utter it, who are so passionately fond of it, that they will scarce admit another into the *embraces* of their lips, which sputter forth a kind of loathing of our *English* language; wherein, if a question be ask'd them, they will, with somewhat of disdain and choler, make answer, *Dim Saisson-ick, i.e.* no English. Their native *gibberish* is usually prattled throughout the whole *Taphydome*, except in their market-towns, whose inhabitants being a little rais'd, and (as it were) puffed up into *bubbles* above the ordinary *scum*, do begin to despise it. Some of these being elevated above the common level, and perhaps refin'd into the quality of having *two suits*, are apt to fancy themselves above their tongue, and, when in their *other cloaths*, are quite ashamed on't. 'Tis usually cashier'd out of gentlemen's houses, there being scarcely to be heard even one single *Welsh* tone in many families; their children are instructed in the *Anglican* idiom, and their schools are *pædagogu'd* with professors of the same; so that if the stars prove lucky) there may be some *glimmering* hopes that *Britih lingua* may be quite extinct, and maybe *English'd* out of *Wales*, as *Latin* was barbarously *Goth'd* out of *Italy*.

The *Cambro-Britons* are great admirers of heroick actions, and much honour the memory of famous atchievements; insomuch, that rather than a *deed-doing* man shall perish in oblivion, they will eternize his name by monument of a *straw*, or some such in considerable trifle; as appears by that famous example of that faint of their country, Bishop *David*, who being a pert fighter, and having foundly *basted* and swaddled their foes, is this day consecrated to posterity by the *trophy* of a leek, and *smells* as rank of renown, from that vegetable *preservative* that embalms his fame, as they do of a *scallion* that carry it: about for his glory. Their hats are set with this anniversary *badge* and emblem of honour, and triumph,. on the first of *March*; which day hath been christened by his name, and, being *dubb'd* an holiday, hath worn yearly in the almanack a *scarlet* letter.

There is *one thing* more also very *observable* among them, and that is, that, of all the maim'd persons that ever we read of, we find none comparable for nimbleness to a *Cambrian cripple*; a pregnant proof whereof was presented to us in this following in stance: A fellow with crutches mov'd by *protusion* in a certain wheel-barrow, espying a bear near the rear of the *thruster*, was so surprized with horror at this tremendous sight, that he pack'd up his *pedestals*, *i.e.* tuck'd his oaken *shins* to the *Zodiack* of his girdle, and away he fled; *Bruin* and the *protusor* in vain troop'd after him, who led them a risk with such winged speed, that they could never overtake him; he clearly outstripp'd them, to the eternal glory and renown of *Welsh lameness*.

These are some of the *choices* observations we made when conversant among the *British* mountains; we might easily have added more (the whole nation indeed being but *one grand remark*) had not the suddenness of our return prevented us. If it should chance to be our lot to set our feet on that soil a second time, we shall venture to present another *show* of it; for 'tis a pity such a rare fight as

Wales should want a *trumpet*, nay, and a *fool* too to proclaim and expose it to the world.

After we had cramm'd our *budget* with these few notices, we jogg'd on with our freight to the brink of the sea, where, *mounted* on a pinnance, we rode to *Bristol*, from whence, with all possible speed, we trudgd in a few days to the *metropolis* of the nation called *London*.

A Trip to North-Wales.
Being a Description of that
Country and People

by

Edward Ward, E. B.

(1701)

To
William Myddleton, *Esq.*;
High Sheriff of *Denbighshire*

Sir,

As it is natural for persons, who have labour'd under misfortunes, and particularly of a similar nature,[1] to have a fellow-feeling for each other, I flatter myself that, as an instance of this disposition, you will favour this address with your notice, and not think it a reason, for denying the following curious collection of travels the honour of your patronage and acceptance.

---

1   Mr. Torbuck was confined in Newgate, last sessions of Parliament, for publishing the debates of the House of Lords and Commons, in 9 vol. octavo.

73

The most learned clerks have always thought it highly for the honour of themselves and their works, to prefix some great name to them, (as they frequently tell us in their epistles of this kind, tho' perhaps they had no other motive in reality than that, which I frankly own, was the occasion of this to you.

And, considering the interest I have in it, what greater name could I have thought of, that could so effectually have promoted it, as that of a person, who has so eminently distinguish'd himself, as the worshipful High Sheriff of *Denbighshire*: A name that shall last as long as the journals of the *British* Parliament and the annals of the *British* nation, and be delivered down to all succeeding times, as an example of publick justice, the terror of venality, and the awe of all future returning officers. As this cannot but be of great emolument to your country, suffer me to congratulate, rather than condole with you, upon your confinement: and give me leave to suppose, however hard-hearted your neighbours of Denbigh may think of you, that you will find some consolation in contributing, tho' sorely against your will, to the utility, to the virtue of posterity.

To make a virtue of necessity, is a part of prudence that you should not want; and therefore I flatter myself, that you are as well reconciled to your present place of abode, as you can be: and as a farther motive to comfort you, you may remember, that if the design of carrying a majority, *om-*

nibus viis & modis, had taken effect, what favour might not a Sheriff have expected, who had acted with so much audacity and vigour in the service of his honour.

> *Aude aliquid brevibus gyaris & carcere dignum*
> *Si vis esse aliquis.————²*

As you cannot fail of being of singular use, in recommending these sheets to the curiosity of the publick, so, be pleased to be assured that I wish your merits may never want their due rewards. I am, with all possible regard,

SIR, Your most obliged, &c.
J. T.

---

2   Latin: Dare to do something worth of exile and prison if you mean to be anybody. (Juvenal). —Ed.

A Trip to North Wales

I know not by what fatality it came to pass, that I was bred up to the study of the law; but, surely the importunity of others had a greater hand in it, than any inclination of my own; for, I was ever of opinion, a young Barrister without an estate (my case) made as awkward a figure, as a Dancing-Master in the habit of a non-con parson; in regard, such rarely get their bread, till they have lost their teeth to eat it. However, being call'd to the bar, I began to consider, what way I might best settle myself into business with the least certainty of expence, and the greatest probability of advantage. Amongst all the numerous projects that fill'd my head, I could think of none like going a *Welsh* circuit: for happening one day (in *Trinity* term) to dine at a *Welsh* judge's house, with whom. I was acquainted, I met there some attornies of that country, who, in less time than a man might say over a *pater-noster*, made all that was set upon the table invisible; and then, to make us amends, entertain'd us with a romantick harangue of the felicities of *North-Wales*, which they talk'd of, as if they had been describing the land of *Promise*, that how'd with milk and honey; nay, they wanted little of persuading me, that broad cloth of twelve shillings a yard grew upon the hedges; and every now and then, a request was wedg'd in, that I would come and practise amongst them. There needed not half to many arguments to put me upon a thing, I was naturally forward enough to undertake. So the bargain was quickly struck up, and I fully determined to visit *Wales* the very next circuit.

But, before I proceed any further, I will first premise some account of the place and inhabitants, and then speak of my own treatment there.

Wales (then anciently called *Cimbria*) is divided into *North* and *South Wales*. 'Tis the former of these I propose to say somewhat of. This consists of six entire, though small, counties, *viz. Montgomery, Flint, Denbigh, Merioneth, Carnarvan*, and the *Isle of Anglesea*, and is separated from *England* by the rivers *Dee* and *Severn*.

The air is the best thing it has to boast of, and will sooner procure you an appetite, than furnish you with means to supply it.

The country looks like the fag end of the creation; the very rubbish of *Noah's* flood; and will (if any thing) serve to confirm an *Epicurean* in his creed, that the world was made by chance.

The highest hills that ever I saw in *England*, such as *Penygent, Ingleborough,* and the like, are meer cherry-stones to the *British* Alps; and no more to be compar'd with them, for stature, than a grashopper with *Goliah* of *Gath.* So that there is not, in the whole world, a people that live so near to, and yet so very far from heaven, as the *Welsh* do.

You cannot travel from town to town, but you must needs take the clouds in your way, who so gratefully resent your civility in calling upon them, that you will have no occasion to complain they send you away dry; for you may, at your journey's end, beshake your cloaths with as good a grace, as any water-dog does his shaggy pantaloons.

A tree challenges as many lookers on here, as a blazing star, or an *African* monster, does elsewhere. And for green things (leeks only excepted) you might have seen as many in *Egypt* when the locusts had been rapareeing the country.

Coaches in many parts were never so much as heard of, nor can the natives form any ideas of them, that are not as disproportioned to the truth, as *Montezuma's* conception of the sea, who had never seen any thing longer than a horse-pond.

Carts are about the size, and somewhat of the shape, of brewers drays.

Horses are no rarities, but very easily mistaken for mastiff-dogs, unless view'd attentively; they will live half a week upon the juice of a flint-stone, (For grass and hay they know as little as oats.) And they will run upon the ridge of a mountain as thin as the back of a knife, with as much security and speed, as an accomplish'd race-horse will exert upon *Newmarket Heath*, or *Salisbury Plain*.

Their beasts are all small, except their women, and their lice, both which are (to an hyperbole) of the largest size.

They want not store of mutton that is tolerably sweet, for meat so lean: but goat's flesh (as more suitable to their own rank constitution) has the preference; this, forsooth, they call *rock-venison*.

These goats are such excellent climbers, that the only way to be familiarly acquainted with them, is to tender your respects, by a musquet-ball.

Little want is there of fish; such as *trout, guinaid, salmon, lobsters*, and the like, but no *maids* to be met with.

Their beef is as tough as an artillery man's coat upon a training day, and requires a very ostrich's stomach to digest it.

You cannot suppose they want pork in a country so very swinish.

Their dressing victuals serves to verify an old proverb, *That where God sends meat, somebody else will furnish them with cooks.*

Their houses generally consist but of one room, but that plentifully stocked with inhabitants; for besides the proprietors, their children, and servants, you shall have two or three swine and black cattle (white they are never without) under the same roof, and hard to say, which are the greater brutes.

These houses have holes dug in their sides, that serve them for a double purpose, both to let in light, and to let out smoak; they represent both windows and chimnies: for, should a man have a chimney perching on the top of his thatched mansion there, he would stand in great danger of being prick'd down for high-sheriff.

Cow-dung is their principal firing; and the neater sort use swine's dung instead of soap.

Necessary houses are the only places reputed needless here: perhaps the same pot that boils their food serves them for another use. This you may assure yourself, there is very soft treading near a *Welsh* house for those that are troubled with corns. In a word, it is an absolute cataplasm; but no carrion will kill a crow.

Thus much for their habitations: now for those that dwell in them.

Some suppose them to be descended from the same common parents with us; but to hear one of them talk, you would take them for a sort of *Pre-Adamites*; nor can there be any thing imagined so troublesome, as a *Welshman*, when possessed with the spirit of genealogy. They are, doubtless, the true offspring of the ancient *Britons*, and have crept into this obscure corner of the world, no ways able to recompense the toil of conquest: they liv'd many ages undisturbed, and as safe as a thief in a mill, till our *Edward*, with much a-do, cudgell'd them into humanity, and persuaded them (fore against their will) to live a little like the rest of their neighbours.

Wolves were formerly as plentiful among them, as pick-pockets at a conventicle, till their princes being obliged to pay a yearly tribute of three hundred: in process of time, no noxious vermin, but the inhabitants, were left in the land.

They have this in common with the *Jews*, that they ever marry in their own tribe, which, as it is detrimental to them, so it is highly advantageous to all others.

Their language is inarticulate and guttural, and sounds more like the gobbling of geese, or turkies, than the speech of rational creatures. It is stuffed as full with aps, as ever you saw a leg of veal with parsley

They are so well vers'd in the history of their descents, that you shall hear a poor beggar woman derive her extraction from the first maid of honour, to *Nimrod*'s wife, or else she thinks she is no-body.

If they want a pewter-spoon or porringer in their house, yet will they by no means be without a pedigree.

The itch is more hereditary among them than estates; and they have lice upon all their bodies. To remedy the former of these inconveniencies, (the other is not reputed any) they anoint themselves so profusely with brimstone, that their shirts and shifts might almost serve instead of card-matches; so that they are intolerable company, if once they get the wind of you.

They are such great lovers of cleanliness, that they never shift above four times a year, and that exactly upon quarter-day, except it happen to be leap-year.

Most of the middle (and all the meaner) sort, are as absolute strangers to shoes and stockings, as to moral honesty, whereby their legs and feet become, in time, so callous, that hardly any thing will hurt them.

For their Christianity (if you'll believe *Tertullian*) they came by it very easily; but, like an old coat, it is now grown so thread-bare, that you can hardly make it out, that there ever was such a thing as Christianity among them.

They preface every thing with *Got* and *St Taphy knows*; which saint was a very worthy gentleman, that could play at back-sword well. You may read of him plentifully in that excellent book, call'd, *The History of the Seven Champions;*[1] to

---

1   Richard Johnson, *The famous history of the seven champions of Christendom St. George of England, St. Denis of France, St. James of Spain, St. Anthony of Italy, St. Andrew of Scotland, St. Patrick of Ireland, and St. David of Wales. Shewing*

which I refer you for further information.

Their most usual imprecations are these; *May hur never wear leek more; May hur be choaked with toasted cheese; and the Tiphill bite hur head off.*

Their churches somewhat resembled the *Jewish* tabernacle converted into a pigeon-house. Their pews look exactly like the pens for geese, calves, and hogs in *Rumford Market*, or *West Smithfield*. And there it is, that (by way of ornament, not use) they deposit those few bibles they have.

Their pulpits (generally the trunk of some hollow tree) are badly covered, and worse lined. Their priests (which are made of the vilest of the people) have just *Latin* enough to entitle them to the benefit of the clergy, and no more. For *Greek*, it suffices them to have heard there is such a thing in the world; they never trouble themselves about it. *Hebrew*, they are the best qualified for that can be partly in regard of their own guttural pronunciation, and partly because it's roots flourish best in barren ground; but they are as absolute strangers to it, as the rest of the uncircumcised world.

---

their honourable battels by sea and land: their tilts, justs, turnaments, for ladies: their combats with gyants, monsters and dragons: their adventures in foreign nations: their enchantments in the Holy Land: their knighthoods, prowess, and chivalry, in Europe, Africa, and Asia; with their victories against the enemies of Christ. Also the true manner and places of their deaths, being seven tragedies: and how they came to be called, the seven saints of Christendom. The first part (London: Ric. Chiswell, M. Wotton, G. Conyers, and B. Walford, 1696). —Ed.

Yet it is rare to see any of them without the rubrick, and *Cambridge* arms, *Lucem* & *pocula*, fire and cups in their faces; so very conformable are they.

The surplices are full as coarse (and almost as white) as carmen's frocks; you would take them for spiritual muckenders, for they are perpetually wiping their noses on them.

Five marks a year will creditably and comfortably maintain one of those illiterate Sir *Johns*, his wife, and fix children; nor do they deserve one penny more than they have. They are universally the sow-gelders and alehouse-keepers of their respective parishes.

I heard a parson recommend, in publick, a woman that had the *French-pox*, first to the mercies of God, in his prayer, next to the charity of all pious well-disposed Christians, that knew not how soon it might be their own condition.

At *Penmorthey*, some of our younger sort sent one evening for a fiddler; and who do you think should come, but the reverend doctor of the parish; who poll's a small squeaking instrument (miscall'd a violin) out of a slit in his cassock, and began to make as good melody as three or four cats in a garret at midnight. A person present threw a cake of butter at him, which so obnubilated one side of his ecclesiastick chaps, he threatened to complain to his diocesan, who was a justice of peace, but was soon stopped by a present of fix pence; a fight, I suppose, he had not been bless'd with since last Easter-offerings. After which, he was so very pliant to the humours of the company, that you might, without offence, have kicked him like a foot-ball.

You may expect, but will not find, any rings of bells here; yet most of their churches have one, about the bigness of a large candlestick, hung upon (not in) a thing like a steeple, as a mushroom is a millpost: this is generally rung out upon any joyful news.

I remember once we had a church-warden's accounts canvass'd in court, and among other things, there are these that follow.

Item, Three pence for a twisted hay-rope to the bell at St *Mary*'s church.

Item, Seven pence for a gate, to keep off *Thomas Ap Richard*'s cow from devouring the aforesaid rope.

Their church-yards serve the dead for a burying, and the living for a dancing-place, and that every Sunday; for there you shall see a blind harper mounted upon a grave-stone, making admirable harmony, surrounded by the long-ear'd tribe, like another *Orpheus* amongst the beasts.

For their civil government, it is after the model of *England*; but, in many things, as much varies from it, as the *Turkish* alcoran does from the *Scotch* directory.

They have judges of their own, that carry with them, in their circuits, an itinerant *Chancery*, *King's Bench*, *Common Pleas*, and *Exchequer*: so that the same hand that inflicts the wound at common law, applies the equity plaister also.

In three weeks time they will sue a man to an out-lawry. It is the form of one of their proclamations; *Morgan Cadwalladar*, Gent. come forth and an-swer to *Jane ap Rice Williams*, in a plea of dower, or else you lose three kine, price fifteen shillings.

They are very favourable to their own country-men, and will by no means subject them to any capital punishment: an instance of which we had in our circuit, where we could not hang one man. There was a fellow indicted for sheep-stealing, and a very pregnant evidence of his guilt produc'd, yet the thick-scull'd jury brought him in guilty of man-slaughter. But strangers are not to expect such fair quarter.

Their civil actions are brought upon very frivo-lous accounts. As for your hens scraping up a dai-sy in your neighbour's garden; for a philip on the role; for saying you are no true *Welshman*, and the like.

No man will appear there, either upon a jury, or a witness, unless he be call'd by his addition of quality, as well as name; as *Hugh Owen*, Esq; *Evan Roberts*, Gent. nay, it has been known, that when my lords the judges have, in their circuits, been so crowded, as to be well nigh stifled upon the bench and the sheriff has found all his mandates to keep the king's peace, upon pain of rebellion, invalid, he has at last been forc'd to cry, All you that are *gen-tlemen of Wales*, and *ancient Britons*, stand off, and keep your distance; which has effectually done the business.

They are of a hot, cholerick temper, and will, upon a word's speaking, run at you with their knives full drive: but as their valour is soon kindled, so it as quickly evaporates.

For their women, they are happy that know them only by report'; for to have to do with them is, in literal sense, to be guilty of the sin of uncleanness.

Reading is a valuable accomplishment amongst both sexes; but, to be able to write too, makes them presently commence rabbies: for many, even of the better fort, think themselves no mean scholar, if they have once attain'd to be able to set their marks to a deed.

Their wenches unspitmeat with their naked teeth, which are full as sweet as clean; so that had *Cornelius Agrippa* seen *Wales*, 'tis more than probable, he had rank'd their cookery amongst his vanities of sciences.

Butter is there of a dark yellowish complexion, mix'd with green; and you must hold your nose in your own defence, before you can put it into your mouth. However, 'tis very good to grease cart wheels.

Eggs bear no price, unless they have chickens in them, and then they are as much coveted, as green pease in *January* by a big-bellied woman, or spiders by a sick monkey.

Toasted cheese epitomizes all dainties with them; and they eat it with as much luxury as the *Scotch* do *steenbarnack*, or the *Irish, bonniclabber*. It is made of cows milk, mixt with that of goats, bitches, and mares; so that an *Englishman* would as soon choose to dine with a hungry *Tartar*, upon sun-burnt horse flesh, as put a bit of it into his mouth.

Forks they never use, looking upon fingers as the more primitive institution.

Their liquor is of a pale deceitful complexion, but as treacherous in it's effects, as the worst of those that either brew or use it.

To sum up their character in one word:

They live lazily and heathenishly; they eat and drink nastily, lodge hardily, snore profoundly, belch perpetually, shift rarely, louse frequently, and smoak tobacco everlastingly.

An account of my entertainment amongst 'em must now ensue.

I had no sooner passed the river *Dee*, but I began to grow sensible I was not in *England*; for the country I was got into, look'd no more like it, than if a man had been in *America*, or the most uninhabited parts of *Arabia*. There was a savage air in the face of every body I met, that plainly told me, these must be descended from *Brutus*, the nephew of *Virgil's* hero.

The first town we stepp'd in, was the *Welsh Pool* in *Montgomeryshire*; where we were so commodiously lodged, that it may be presum'd *Marius*, when in she *Feus Minturnum*, lay in a palace, when compar'd with this ill-favour'd resemblance of an inn. We got, early to bed, in regard of next day's journey, which consisted of twelve *Welsh* (that is to say thirty-six *English*) miles;[2] for every one of them was a complete Dutch league.

I had not gone above a third part of the my horse lost a shoe, an ordinary misfortune in that rocky country. I desired the judge to stay till he was shod, but he told me he could not, for he was oblig'd, by such an hour, to meet his brother at the city of *Dinas Mouthaye* (a place I shall no more forget, than a parliament soldier *Edgehill* or *Marsten Moor*) which, as he said, lay strait on, and was but six miles distant. I order'd my man to book it down, to prevent mistakes; and expected to find a place, at least, twice as big as *Shrewsbury*. Well, I got my beat shod, with much ado, by as very a beast as himself; a smith that could speak no more *English* than a dromedary, and work'd at least three fathom under ground, like the ancient *Troglodites Herodotus* and *Strabo* mention.

The first object I met, I had like to have mistook for a piece of *German* clock-work; his head, hands, and feet, all kept time; whilst he put himself to no less pains than Hercules in cleansing the Augean stables, to make a living *Automaton*, call'd a *keffel*, or horse, move. The creature appear'd thoroughly to have imbib'd the doctrine of passive obedience, and no more valued his rider's stripes and kicks, than the *French* king does the Duke of *Modena*; but still preserv'd, in his pace, a majes-

---

2   The Welsh mile (*milltir* or *milldir*) was 3 miles and 1,470 yards long, or 6.17 km. It comprised 9,000 paces (*cam*), each of 3 Welsh feet (*troedfedd*) of 9 inches (*modfeddi*). —Ed.

tick *Spanish* gravity: it look'd as if he had lineally descended from *Praisa God bare bones*, and was so gross an idolater, that almost every moment it bowed down to stocks and stones. Friend, says I, which is the way to the city of *Dinas Mouthaye*? He survey'd me with as great attention, as if he designed to draw my picture, for a full quarter of an hour; and then comforted me with a *Diggon Comrague, Dimfarsnick, i.e.* (as I was afterwards told) *I can speak* Welsh *but no* English. At last, riding on (after not a few perplexing fears), I was got into the middle of the city, enquiring the way to it; till a woman, that had shoes and stockings on (whom, for that reason, I took to be a person of quality) told me I was in the high-street. Casting my wonder-struck eyes about here and there, by some half pikes, that over-topp'd a small cottage, I began to perceive my judge was got into his grandeur, and so it prov'd.

I found him in the uppermost room of the house (that had, notwithstanding, a clay floor) which was hung with as noble and elegant tapestry as ever spider's room produc'd.

The porridge-pot (bold as it was) fac'd his majesty's prime commissioners of *Oyer* and *Terminer*, without the least appearance of shame; but the broom, as if good housewifery were quite out of countenance, was modestly retir'd in a corner, behind the door. It had two beds at the upper end, a goat and two pigs at the lower end, and a fire-place in the middle. His lordship bad me welcome, and told me I came in padding time, for they were just going to dinner, and stay'd only for Mr Mayor: Ay, thought I, it must needs be a blessed Mayor that belongs to this corporation; and in the midst of my contemplations, his worship was pleas'd to appear.

There was a fellow that carried a battoon, or truncheon (daub'd with yellow at each end, in imitation of gilding) much of the same fashion with those the marshals of the city militia carry before their captains, instead of a mace before him.

He was of a presence sufficiently august and venerable, for he had just such a face as our sign post daubers give King *Harry* VIII. of glorious memory; and it might be divided, as Dr *Heylin* has done the kingdom of *Poland*, into wood-land and champaign: the nethermost part was lamentably over-grown with hair, which much resembled *Bafat* a baker. His hat might be worth about two groats,[3] for the kitchen stuff that was on it; but setting aside that, the whole inventory of his wearing apparel had been over-rated at six-pence. His cloaths hung about him like bandileers or sau-

---

3   The groat is the traditional name of a defunct English and Irish silver coin worth four pence. First minted under King Edward I, the immediate ancestor to the groat was the French *gros tournois* or groat of Tours. From the reigns of Charles II to George III, it was minted irregularly and was largely known as fourthpence. Initialy it had 90 grains (5.8 g) of sterling silver, but the weight was progressively reduced until it reached 32 grains (2.1 g) in 1559, following which, it was not minted again until Charles II. In the United Kingdom it ceased to be minted in 1865. —Ed.

sages, and to speak the truth, he was the raggedest dog of a magistrate that ever my eyes beheld.

However, the judges gave him the right-hand of fellowship, and set him up at the upper end of the table, where, after a little of the *Welsh* ale had invaded his *pericranium*, his tongue run as nimbly as wild-fire, and that so very long, that the philosophers, who were at a loss for a perpetual motion, might have found it there.

I remember (amongst other things) pointing to a house over the way, that the sun shone through in about five and forty places (and where one would have thought a dog, or a cat, could not have subsisted a fortnight without catching cold) *Got knows* (says my old gentleman) *hur family has flourish'd there these eleven hundred years.*

From thence we departed, after dinner, for the town of *Dolgelthlie*, in *Merioneththire*, where we kept our first assizes, or (to speak in their language) great sessions.

In our passage, upon the brow of a mountain, we were met by the high-sheriff, at the head of the gentry: they were such as would hardly have pass'd muster, for petty constables here; but there it was every one, colonel such-a-one, and justice such-a-one. They were mounted upon little keffels, about a cubit and half high, to which a *Scotch* galway, or *Irish* garron, look'd like *Bucephalus* himself; but what they wanted in stature, was abundantly supply'd with the length of mane and tail, and a deep channel between every brace of ribs.

This town of *Dolgelthlie*, had several things very remarkable belonging to it; of which, the most memorable were these.

First, It was wall'd with walls six miles high, meaning a ridge of rocks that environ'd it: and they were such, I'll assure you, as would have bid defiance to *Hannibal* and all his vinegar.

Then we came into it under water, and out of it over water. A boarded channel convey'd a small river over our heads; and we went out of it over a bridge, *Moxe Anglicano*.

Then the steeple grew. There was but one bell, a mere tintinnabulum, and that hung in a tree, which, to do the country right, was the only tree I saw-growing there: for, setting aside that, I did not see living timber enough to make a whipping-post of.

Lastly, There were more ale-houses: than houses in it; for every house was subdivided into divers little tenements, each of which sold drink apart.

Surrounded by a vast tribe of the bare-footed regiment, we got, at length, to our lodgings; where I desired my landlady to show me a good room: *That shall you have*, says she, *Got knows: And such a one Christ nor St David ever lodged in.* And in that the spoke nothing but truth; for it was a ground chamber, whose walls looked as if they had catch'd the leprosy. They were plaister'd with mortar of twenty different sorts of colours; and at the bed's head was a cranny, through which the wind diluted with force enough to blow off a man's night-cap.

No less than a whole cart-load of monumental timber was carv'd into my bed-stead; and it was to be ascended by a ladder of six or eight steps, so that it was highly necessary for a man to make his will before he went into it, left, if he had tumbled out in the night, he had awaked in another world the next morning, as infallibly he must have done.

The ticking was so obdurate, that it seemed to be quilted with flint-stones instead of feathers; and perfectly drew indentures in my flesh.

Upon the tester, a whole race of *Welsh* spiders, descended, as I presume, from the great *Cadwallader*, hung in clusters, ready to drop into my mouth, if I slept with it open.

I had a pair of sheets laid on as coarse as any nutmeg-grater: I wish, to my comfort, I could have said they had been half as clean; for they look'd of as dimsy a complexion, as if they had scrubb'd half the keffels, or horses, in the country with them. When I expressed my dissatisfacton, and told my landlady, I did, at least, depend upon the civility of a pair of clean sheets, as being us'd to wear pretty good linnen: she reply'd, *Got knows, I need not be so nice; they had not been lain in but six or eight weeks; she took them fresh off her husband's bed.* And then, you know, I had no reason to complain.

Well—in I got, but could no more sleep, than if I had been in *Regulus*'s barrel, or little ease; for I had a regiment or two of fleas immediately at free quarter upon me; which prov'd such admirable phlebotomists, that I hardly knew myself next morning, when I came to consult a looking-glass. And they may talk what they will of their black cattle, I am sure I found some of a different complexion next morning; and, in a week's time, I was grown so complete a grazier, that I could have stock'd e'er a Tartar, in the country. My judge lodg'd in some what a better room over-head; and following him down stairs one day, I had the luck to find an over-grown louse of the first magnitude, on his scarlet jobes. I was at first strongly tempted to lay violent hands on it, for it's audacity; but at last resolved to let it alone; concluding it must needs, some time on other, fall into the hands of judice; as no doubt bat it did, though unknown to me.

My man they cramm'd into a hole in the roof of the house, the hieroglyphick of an oven, much about the size of an *English* hen-roost; where, not-withstanding, as he told me himself, he made a shift to enjoy a more comfortable repose than his master could meet with.

But this was not all: misfortunes rarely come single: in the middle of the night (wanting the usual fortifications of lock and bolt to my cham-ber-door) in comes a great low, who, I suppose, had been tenant in possession there before, and came to claim a re-entry. She was so very big, that I was horribly afraid she would have pigg'd un-der my bed: with this grunting chamber-fellow I was oblig'd to pass over the night, but never in my whole life before pray'd either so heartily, or so of-ten, *Phosphore redde diem.*

Next morning, occasionally consulting a bit of looking-glass that was pasted up against the wall (in which a pigmy could not see his phiz, but by *synechdoche*) I found I was grown an absolute stranger to my own countenance, so miserably had my cannibals excoricated and disfigur'd it.

When I got up I call'd for a bason of water, to see if the liquid element would contribute any thing towards meliorating my looks. The wench (to shew the frankness of her temper) brings no less than a pail full, but so very dirty, that (excepting her own face) I saw nothing likelier to turn a man's stomach in a morning fasting. All that I shall say of my towel is, that it was very correspondent to my sheets.

I next sent out for a barber (resolving to set the best face upon matters I could) and, in about half an hour's time, in comes a greasy fellow, swift to shed innocent blood, who, in a trice, from a portable cupboard, call'd his cod-piece, pulls out a woollen night-cap that smelt very much of human sweat and candle-grease, and about two ells of toweling, of so coarse a thread, that they might well have serv'd a zealous catholick instead of penitential hair-cloth.

After some fumbling, he pulls out a thing he call'd a razor, but both by the looks and effects, one would easily have mistaken it for a chopping-knife; and with pure strength of hand, in a short time, he shav'd me so clean, that not only the hairs of my face, but my very skin was become invisible;

for he left me not sufficient to make a patch for an *Æthiopian* lady of pleasure: I gave him a small piece, bearing *Cæsar*'s image and superscription; at which, he doffed me so low a bow, that the very clay floor was indented with his knuckles, and so he reverendly took his leave.

Going into the kitchen, which was as near my chamber as might be, I found my landlady preparing for a very nice piece of cookery, and that was to make a fricasee of chickens, by the help of a whistle that summon'd also her maids and hogs. The young family were soon got to the rendezvous; and when she saw a full appearance, a good billet, artificially manag'd, made the *mittimus* of about half a dozen of them in a moment's space; both their feathers and skin were stripp'd, and the poor creatures handled with more barbarity, than a *London hangman* ever us'd a traitor's body.

Whilst I stood in a brown study, contemplating her neatness, I was on a sudden surpriz'd with a noise, much resembling that of coopers, trunk-makers, pewterers, and tinkers, in concert: in a word, *Babel* itself never produc'd a more confus'd or inharmonious jargon.

Upon putting my head out of the window, I found it was a company of their militia, marching into a valley to perform their exercise: they did so exceedingly revive in my memory the Black-Guards, that I was some time before I could persuade myself I was not at *Charing Cross*.

They went, as the unclean beasts enter'd the

ark, by couples; most of them had swords stuck in the waistband of their breeches, for want of more regular belts; they had quires of brown paper stitch'd upon their stomachs, to keep off bullets; and about two-thirds of them were arm'd with birding-pieces, as if they were going to make war with the sparrows, field fares, and jackdaws; the rest carried long poles, miscall'd pikes: their colours seem'd to be patch'd together out of some old *Darneux* curtains; what their impress was I could not learn. Their drums were pails and small tabs, headed with pedigrees, which made a terrible noise; their officers, for distinction, instead of scarves and croslets, wore great bunches of leeks in their hats. When their names were call'd over, you would have concluded you had heard the muster-roll of *Xerxes*'s army, but 'twas only, *Vox,* & *præterea nihilia.*

As I cast my eyes around, I espied an object, that methought (in regard of his rueful looks, and wretched habit) were intitled to compassion, if not charity; and he seem'd, with a very moving, though dumb rhetorick, to invite me to a conference; but, bless me! how easily are we mortals mistaken? This very individual numerical animal, who was the absolute hieroglyphick of a scarecrow, instead of asking me an alms, as I verily expected, came to proffer me a fee, or rather bribe; for it seems, some malicious neighbours of his had a month's mind to make him high sheriff of the county, he being a substantial gentleman, worth sixty pounds *per annum,* and he was desirous to use my supposed interest with the judges to get him excus'd.

Thus was I introduc'd into the circuit; what further memorable passages did occur in, and out of court, I design, if this meets with a friendly reception, to make the subject of a second part, and so for the present shall give a little repose to my pen and fingers-ends.

A Funeral Sermon,
Preached by the
Parson of Langwillin

Kulott inv.t et Fecit,

early peloved prethren; I am here among you to make a creat preachment upon a tead body: my text is in the ten and twentieth chapter of the *Macabes*, the ferse, indeed, I cannot very well remember, but I am sure it was there; the words are these, *Figitate* & *orate*, that is to say, Watch and pray. I will stick to my text, I will warrant you: Our creat-crand-father *Adam* was a fery cood old man, inteet, inteet, truth he was, and lif'd in Cod's own house, in paradise, a fery fine place, I will warrant you; he had all things profided to his hands, he needed not to puy a spoon or a nocking, he hat all sorts of trees, as plumb-trees, pear-trees, sherry-trees, and codling-trees, but for want of cood-take-heed, hur was fall. Our creat-crand-mother Efe, a pox take her for a plague, pago must needs go rop an orchard, the Tephil shew'd hur the way, for there is no mischief on foot, but the Tephil and the woman must hafe a finger in the pie; so hur was come home, and persuade hur husband to eat some of hur stolen apple, it was Cod's mercy it did not stick in hur throat and choak him: after this, she was profe with child, and prought to pet of prafe poy, and call hur name, I cannot fery well remember—Oh, *Cain*; yea, *Cain*; it was this prafe poy, but unluck rogue, like hur mother: after this, hur was prought to ped of nother prafe poy, and call hur name *Apel*, oh, that was cood lad; and now I come to part with my text; hur was pray, and had hur watch too, pefore Cod, hur prother *Cain* had not come pehind her pack and knock hur prains out; this was murthering fillan, so hur was forced to out-run hur country, and so into a strange land, which taught hur strange tricks: O this sin of murther, my peloved, prought heafy fudgment upon the earth, and what do you think it was? I will tell you then, It prought these lawyers and pum-pailiffs, to rop the people of their estate and money; after this my pelofed, was come another sin upon the earth, and prought heafier shudgment along with-it, and what do you think that was? I will tell you then, it prought these consuming catpillers, these destroying locusts, these hellish vermin, join'd together with excisemen and custom-house officers, to pry into every nook; and look into every corner for trop of cood trink marry; Cod confound them all, and from them, *libera nos Domine*, that is to say, *Cood Lord deliver us*: my pelofed, peware, I peceech, of this loathsome fine of trunkenness, for our creat-crand-father *Noah* had no sooner scape scouring in the ark, and cot safe to land acain, put he went to the first ale house he could find, and there was trink, trink, trink all day, and all night, and then come home trunk, and puse hur family, so I doubt it is with to many of you: my pelofed, at the treadful day of shugement, when the pastors shall becall'd to gife an account of the sheep delifer'd to their sharge, and when the poor unworthy parson of *Langwillin* shall be call to gife an account for the sheep to delifer to my charge,and when the Lord call, I will not hear; and when hur call again, I will not answer; and when hur call a third time, I will say as old *Ely* bid *Samuel* say, Lord, speak, thy servant heareth thee; and when he ask me for the sheep delifer'd to my sharge, pefore Cod I will tell him flat and plain, you are all turn'd coats, (*i.e.*) goats.

EPITAPH on a COBLER, buried
    in *Edmonton* Church-yard.

Hic jacet *Newberry Will*,
Qui Vitam finivit cum Cochiæ Pill.
Quis administravit? *Bellamy Su*.
Quantum Quantitatis? Nescio, Scisne Tu?

Ne Sutor ultra Crepidam.

The Welshman's Warning-Piece,
as it was Deliver'd in a
Sermon in Shropshire

by

Shon ap Morgan

oot People, 'tis written in the Pook of Kot, I cannot twas tell well where; put hur I'cannot tell well where; put hur 'twas tere, *Vishilata torata*, that is much as to say in hur Mutter Tongue, *Wash and Pray*, wella go too, ten hur must liver hur Text out of te Pook of Kot, hur said pefore hur cannot tell where, put hur was warrant hur, hur was tere: *Attam*, Fater *Attam* was coot old Man was warrant hur, must use told seperation, pecause acree pest wid te *Creek* and *Eprue*: *Attam*, Fater *Attam* was plasht in Paradise, Kor's nown House, prave House, prave Plashe, nay hur warrant hur 'twas a sweet plashe, where was all manner of prave Tings, all manner prave Tree, Appol-tree, Pum-tree, Fig-tree, Pere-tree, eye all manner of Tree; yet *Attam* was fall, eye and how was *Attam* fall, *Attam* was fall upon *Heva*, and how was *Attam* fall upon *Heva*, for lack of coot take heed: Terefore take heed how you fall upon *Heva*, tar is, how you fall on your Vences, your prave Guls, your painted Punts; for take heed to *Vihilata torata*, Wash and Pray, was warrant hur keep her Text ftill. *Heva*, Moder *Heva* was plasht tere too, *Heva*, Moder *Heva* was spy Appol on a Tree, a Pock on hur fur Lapour, *Heva* eat Appol, *Heva* gave Appol to At tam, to Fader *Attam*, to deceive coor old Man, Pock on hur again for hur Lapour: Coot People take heed of *Heva*, for *Heva* tid receive coot Fader *Attam*, and all Woman do still receive Man.

Terefore hur say acain and acain, *Vishilata torata*, Wash and Pray, hur warrant hur keep hur Text still.

Lot, old Fader *Lot*, was cood old Man too, had too Wences, two pretty Wences to hur Taughters: *Lot* made Wine, *Lot* tid trink Wine, and Lot was trunk. And how was *Lot* trunk? Why, wid trinking of Wine: Coot People take heed of trinking of Wine, tho it is sweet, for Trunkenness is a creat Sinne. What tid *Lot* peloved when he was trunk, tid he sleep, no, her tid lye with poth hur nown Taughters, Opominable Ting; nay *Lot* tid get hur two Taughters we shild, which was very nought; and why tid hur so, for want of Grace, Vishilata torata, Wash and Pray, hur warrant hur keepe hur Text ftill.

Taffie, Taffie, hur nown Country-man was porn in *Monmouthshire,* neer te Creek of te well, was first Man plaid Welch Harp was prave King, and *Saul,* was a mighty King, but *Taffie* was wise King; yet *Taffie* fell? Taffie was fell upon *Persepa:* O how was *Taffie* fell upon *Persepa?* for lack of coot take heed; terfore take heed *Visilata torata,* Wash and Pray, I warrant hur keep hur text still.

Shobe that holy and shaft Man, *Shobe* had mush Oxe, mush Alle, mush Sheep, mush Cowe, mush Calfe, mush Camel, creat House, mush Shimney, yea mush all Tings; yet shuft Man *Shobe* was fall too, and how was shust Man *Shobe* fall ? te Tiphill took hur, threw hur town, preft hur and mush Shabe, mush Boyl, mush Sore, mush all Sickness, a Pock on te Tiphill for hur Lapour, have no coot will remain for te shust Man *Shobe*: Terefore if te shuft Man *Shobe* was fall, hur had need take heed what hur do and what hur say, *Vishilata torata, Wash and Pray*, I warrant hur keep bur Text still.

Tus you see, coot People, how tat *Attam* was fell, Heva was fell, *Lot* was sell, *Taffie* was fell, shust Man *Shobe* was fell, yea all was tell: And how was all fell? All was fell from Kot to the Tiphell, from Heaven to Hell, tat prave Plasse, to Hell tat foul stinking Plasse: Terefore *Vishilata torata, Wash and Pray*, hur warrant hur keep hur Text still.

Tere are many more in te Pook of Kot tat was fell too, *Absolam* was fell, and how was *Absolam* fell? He was fell upon *Damar* his nown Sister,

Shaul was fell, and how? to Idlerry. A creat deal more was fell too, put hur cannot name chem, put tey pe in te Pook of Kot, and, as hur said pefore, hur cannot tell where, put tere tey be hurs sure; *Vishilata torata, Wash and Pray*, hur warranc hur keep hur Text still.

Prethren and Sisters, hur hope tat none of you will pe offended at hur Preachment, and say hur peaks well, put hur Words and Actions acree not: Hur cannot shustifie hurself, hur was likewise fall too, and hur was have creat many Faults, put hur cive Kot Tanks, hur has always pin coverned py a cood Spirit, and my Toctrine hath civen coot Content unto most of you: Hur has not pin proud, tat ye all know, hur might have pin a Beshit, put hur cive Kot Tanks, hur had more Crace, and had rather make a Preachment here in a Tub, tan in te Tower. Terefore hur shall make use of hur Text and *Vishilata torata, Wash and Pray*, ta ther come not in tat Place, hur warrant hur keep hur Text still. But hur must now come to make some uses.

Peloved People, you must first take heed of Curosity, or hur will pe trown out of Paradise, out of dat prave Plasse, dat sweet Plasse, *Vishilata torata, Wash and Pray*, hur warrant hur keep hur Text still.

Secondly, Take heed of peing trunk, for fear dat te Tiphill catch hur, and so hur never come acain to see hur Friends and Countrymen. *Vishilata torata, Wash and Pray*, hur warrant hur keep hur Text still.

Thirdly, Take heed of Whoring, for tat is a creat Sinne and will pring you to te Tiphill, put *Vishilata torata, Wash and Pray*, hur warrant hur keep hur Text still.

Terefore, coot People, take heed, and tink of hur Preachment, and contemn not te Advice of te Man of Kot, for if hur do, Kot will plague hur in tis World, and in te World to come. *Vishilata torata, Wash and Pray*, her warrant her keep hur Text still.

Tus Peloved hur may see wat creat Danger tis to pe Trunkerds, Horemasters, and inteed to pe nought: pe coot Fellows, put not trunk; love Woman, put not Hores; live honestly and Kot will plesse ye. So for tis Time hur has ton; for hur tink tat Tinner is almost ready, to which Kot pring hur for Mercy fake, *Amen*.

The
Welsh School-Master:
Being Some
Natural Observations Made in the
School of Llandwwfwrhwy

by

R. P. During His Residence There

Llandwwfwrhwy, March 1, 1708.

SIR,

eeing your papers communicated to the publick in the most in genious Transactions of the *Royal Society*; and being fir'd, I hope, or rather presume, with a desire and expectation of equal glory, I recollected that saying of Mr *Cowley*,

Tentanda via est, qua me quoque possim tollere humo.

And thence, upon serious recollection of past accidents of my life, I thought it might not be unuseful to posterity, nor to mankind at present, to give an account of what happened to me since I first came to be a school-master.

In the memorable year 1688, being an hundred years after the *Spanish Invasion*, and twenty years before this present year, as may appear by the most exact calculation, a person, whose goodness is greater than my deserts, preferr'd me to the school of *Llandwwfwrhwy*: at my coming to the town, I found persons of all sorts and sexes, men, women, and children; and that day (as I shall always remember) there was a woman brought-to-bed of seven live children, which dying soon after, were put into a tray, being half boys and half girls, *viz.* three boys and three girls, and one hermaphrodite. I could not but wonder how persons should be so prolifick, in so barren a place; for the town was surrounded with large mountains, nor did you *come into it any way upon arable land*; for there is but one way to the town or parish, and that was not convenient for a coach and six horses to turn in. This is all expressed in the very name of Llandwwfwrhwy, for w is significant of a mountain, and the more w's there are in a town's name, the more mountains about it. Now there are few towns in *Wales* without a *w*. The name of the very country itself beginning with it, shews it to be the predominant letter of the nation. Now w in this town's name being four times multiplied into itself, produces w four, or the fourth power of the root w, which is equal to w. Mountains quadratically multiplied into w. Mountains which makes a power of mountains. The word *Llan* is the same that the *Scotch* and *Irish* pronounce *Clan*, which signifies a company of people of the same lineage; and, indeed, I found in this town, not only all of them a-kin each to the other, but likewise to all *Welshmen* besides: and, which most surprized me, as they said, were all gentlemen. The word *dwarf* is not unlike in sound and signification to the English word *tuff, ruff, gruff*. The word rwbwy is likewise the same as the *English* word *crooked* or *awry*, so that the pedigree of the name of *Llandwwfwrhwy* being thus explained, it appears to be a town encompassed with mountains, with a rough crooked way leading to it.

These mountains *seem to be nothing else but a* composition of such hard, rocky, marmoreous, flinty, lapideous, stony, scopulous, torry, cretaceous, obdurate, petrifactory, intractable, indissoluble; and, in a word, mountainous matter, as the Deluge could not carry, nor the rains, for many infinite numbers of years, although (*gutta cavat lapidem*) be able to penetrate, nor, indeed, cause such an impression upon them, as they might become fit for plowing or pasturing.

Now speaking of mountains, I cannot but take notice, that amongst them is a sort of animal that is neither sheep nor cow, but serves the inhabitants instead of both; it is endued with gravity, and bearded like a philosopher, from it's infancy, its favour is of the rankest, and its manners inclined to voluptuousness; it ascends those mountains with great facility, without any help of stairs or ladder, even to the utmost summit, where it's owner dares not follow, and a telescope is wanting to survey it's proportion; it is very moderate in it's diet, and lives upon much less than a maid and cat at board wages; so that, in that point, I can compare it to nothing but a hackney horse, that is left to feed upon rack staves, or some of my acquaintance and yours, that will flea a flint upon occasion. The sides of some of these mountains are not impervious by art with such instruments as pick-axes, maundrills, sledges, iron crows, spades, and such like things: within the veins lies a bituminous, sulphureous and opake fort of brittle stones, combustible, inflammable; which being carried first in wheel-barrows, and afterwards in carts, to the town, is by the inhabitants called pit-coal, with which the most industrious young gentlewomen of the family generally makes a fire, which serves for many uses, as warming their fingers in winter, brewing their ale, seldom for washing their linnen, sometimes for toasting their noses, but daily for toasting their cheese. Wood faggots are scarcer here than at *Bath* or *Northampton*; I have seen some fruit trees in the adjoining vallies, particularly one, whose deliciousness is protected with many ringent excrescences, and its fruit is black when 'tis red, and red when 'tis green: there are several trees of above a foot high,which bear a plum called *drumwbyddyth*, almost as good, if not the same, as you and the North Britains call a Now, or a flee:

ashes, elms, oaks and crab-trees we have none, so that we have no conveniency of a gallows nearer than *Chester*. As for our grass, it is as long as that upon any of your heaths whatsoever; and for hay it is just enough to frighten a fat ox, *dry up a milch cow, and starve a horse*. One thing I must further observe to you, that within the parish, about half a mile from the church, is a pretty farm called *Llandavie*, where formerly St *David's* ancestors lived; it is composed of sand, broken stones, gravel and rubbish, brought, as we suppose, from the neighbouring hill: the ancient edifice consists of one large room, in which there is an apartment for the gentry, divided by several furze faggots from the offices, where usually lodge a poney, a cow, and a calf, and two milch goats, when they are so civil to come home, for calling for. The whole *farm is a thousand nine hundred yards in compass, and sixteen, eighteen, and twenty yards in breadth: 'tis scarce conceivable how considerable a rent it yields to the Lord Ap Noah*, whose ancestors purchased it from the Lord *Ap Methusalem*. But to come more properly to my own habitation, in the school of which, next under her Majesty, I am supream head and governor: it was built, or rather hewed, out of a rock, by *Raynar*, alias *Morgan Dha*, that is the good Morgan in the days, and by the command of the *Patriarch Enoch Dha*; all the damage it sustained by the Flood, was contracting some damp; but *Japhet* knowing what *Wales* was, sent his eldest son *Price ap Japhet*, who coming there, endowed the school with twenty chaldron of coals yearly, which noble benefaction does, or at least should, still continue. Since the Flood there have been four hundred and sixty-six, and I am the four hundred and sixty-seventh master. Before the Flood, they living long, there were but two, *Price ap Evan Dha* the good, and *Davie ap Shones Gorma*, or the naughty; in whose time the Flood came: so that, by adding two to four hundred and sixty-seven, if I am not mistaken, I am the four hundred and sixty-ninth master from *Raynar*, alias *Morgan Dha* the founder, and God bless him, and *Price ap Japhet* too.

When I came to the school, I found but four that could read without book, and never a-one but one that could write, and he could not write neither, for he had neither pen, ink, nor paper, nor his father before him; but I, and my usher, who is my wife, by great industry, increased my school to six, all the most considerable persons of the parish sending their sons and daughters to us; so that then I had two that could read fair, that could not read, and never a-one that could write; and, by the mathematicks, it's easy to calculate how much they improved: it is remarkable, I had never a scholar under two years old, nor any much more than thirty, though I have in other places known several that have been upwards of forty. As my scholars were preferred to shoes and stockings, they went off; so that, as I remember, at one triennial visitation of the Bishop's, the school-master of *Llandwwf-*

wrhwy being called, was asked by the Bishop how many scholars he had? I answered, I had none; for, by great industry, I had so accomplished them, that their parents, by my advice, according to their capacities, had thought fit to provide for them in the bordering counties, some to feed sheep, and some to steal them.

Near this town is the finest garden in the world; for it is most productive of leeks, and those the most redolent: it is the ancient garden of *St David*; from whence he took the victorious leeks, with which his soldiers were crowned. To this day it is enclosed with a natural stone wall, upon which is this inscription:

Dwyth, Lwyd, Dwynnyth,
Llwyd, Dlwyth, Whynnyth,
Whynnyth, Llwyd, Whyn,
Llwyd, Whynnyth, Gwynn,
Gwynn, Dwynnyth, Whyth,
Whynnyth, Llwyd, Dwyth.

It is observable, that in this inscription there are but eight letters, but each of them, by the different placing of words, is significant of several things; from which I think it is plainly demonstrable, that in St David's time the *Welsh* had only these eight letters, D, G, H, L, N, T, W, Y, one of which letters, *viz.* H, is generally said to be no letter, so that we cannot positively affirm these eight letters to be more than seven, and that the rest have been add-

ed unnecessarily by the superfluity and luxurious-
ness of after ages, to express such habits, diet, and
utensils, as were unknown to the ancient *Britons*. I
think I may not have injured them by the following
tranlation:

Come Britons, come, and each receive
Such verdant leek as tempted Eve,
Transplanted here from paradise,
'Twill safely make ye brave and wise:
'Tis with this scent we will oppose
The sweetness of the English rose.

I design you a second; in the mean time, *Vale,
Vir doctisime, & Societatem summam qua decet
observantia meo Nomine saluta.*

Tuus per omnes Casus,

R.P.

Muscipula:
or, The Mouse-Trap.
A Poem

WRITTEN IN LATIN
BY E. HOLDSWORTH, OF MAGD. COLL. OXON

MADE ENGLISH
BY SAMUEL COBB, M. A. LATE OF
TRINITY COLLEGE, CAMBRIDGE

―――――――――*Inhuman Men ,*
Skillful in Guile and Mischief, have contriv'd
A dire Machine, full of insidious Fraud,
They call a TRAP, a mortal Foe to MICE.
                                        Homer's *Batr.*

1743

Muscipula,
sive
Kambro-Myo-Maxia

Monticolam *Britonem*, qui primus vincula *muri*
    Finxit, & ingenioso occlusit carcere furem,
    Lethalesque dolos, & inextricabile fatum,
Musa refer. Tu, *Phæbe* potens, (nam te quoque quondam
Muribus infestum dixerunt *Smynthea* vates)
O! faveas; & tot *Cambrorum* è montibus, unum
Accipiens vice *Pindi*, adsis, dum pingere versu
Res tenues, humilique juvat colludere Musâ.

The Mouse-Trap.
A Poem

ing, MUSE, the BRITON, who on
    mountains bred,
And like *Saturnian* Jove, with goat's
    milk fed,
In the close prison of a wiry house,
By magic cunning, first incag'd a *mouse*;
Notorious felon, the dire charms relate
Which hurry'd on inextricable fate;
And thou, O PHÆBUS, if that sound delight
Thy willing ear, to aid the Poet's flight,
Or rather SMYNTHEUS thy attention claim,
To ancient *mice* a formidable name:
Now in my breast let all thy favour throng,
And guide me in this unattempted song.

Mus, inimicum animal, prædari, & vivere rapto
Suetum, impunè diu, spolii quà innata libido
Jufferat, erravit, sceleratam exercuit artem
Impavidus, saliensque hinc illinc, cuncta maligno
Corrupit dente, & patinâ malè lusit in omni.
Nil erat intactum, sed ubique domesticus hostis
Assiduus conviva aderat, non mœnia furtis
Obstare, aut vectes poterant servare placentas,
Robustæ fores; quà non data porta, peredit
Ipse sibi introitum, dapibusque indulsit inemptis.

Pestis at hæc totum dum serpsit inulta per orbem,
Cambria præcipuè flevit, quia *cafeus* illic
Multus olet, quem *mus* non, æquè ac plurima, libat,
Aut leviter tantùm arrodit, sed dente frequenti
Excavat, interiùsque domos exculpit edules.

Forsake thy wonted *Pindus*, to descend
From *Cambrian* mountains, and my toil befriends
While I, delighted with the talk, rehearse
Small actions, painted in heroic verse.

    A *mouse*, a creature of that savage kind,
Whom nature form'd with a voracious mind,
Had long, unpunish'd, by successful toil
Flourish'd on rapine, and grown rich with spoil:
Secure he rang'd, and, like a villain, ply'd,
Where hunger prompted, and where laws deny'd,
By quick excursions on each dish he prey'd.
And spoil'd the viands where his teeth were laid.
The nimble rover, at each private feast,
Intruded boldly, an unbidden guest.
Not towers of brass, nor doors of steel cou'd bar
The greedy tyrant from incroaching war.
Cheese-cakes and tarts, to stop his raging lust,
Were fortify'd in vain with brittle crust.
With unbought victory his arms were crown'd,
He found no bars, or eat through what he found.

    But while o'er all the world this poison crept,
Which, unreveng'd, the desolation wept.
WALES chiefly mourn'd the ruinous disease,
A nation fam'd for valour, and for *cheese*;
Cheese, the consummate dish, and found delight
For which alone a *mouse* would *custards* slight.
For those by fits, with nice and careless play,
He licks, and wantons in the milky way.
But *cheese* supplies him with a double
At noon to riot, and at night retreat,
And be at once his lodging, and his meat.

Gens tota incensa est super his, rabiesq; dolorque
Discruciant animos, frendent, juga summa pererrant,
Stare loco ignorant, nam *Cambris* prona furori
Corda calent, subitâque ignescunt pectora bile,
Cum digitis, credas animos quoque *sulphure* tinctos.

Ergò, jubente irâ, dignas cum sanguine pœnas
Sumere decretum est, sed quâ ratione latronem
Tam cautum illaqueent, quo vindice furta repellant
Incertum; neque *felis* enim tua, *Cambre*, tueri
Tecta, nec adversis poterat succurrere rebus.
Illa quidem varias posuit circum ora cavernæ
Insidias, tacitoque pede ad cava limina repens
Excubias egit; frustrà: mus nempe pusillo
Corpore securus, tantò & præstantior hoste
Quo minor, intentum prædæ si forte videret
Custodem autem fores, retro irruit, inque recessus
Aufugit curves, atque invia *felibus* antra:
Inde caput metuens iterùm proferre, nec ausus
Excursus tentare novos, nisi caftra moverer
Prædo, atq; omne aberat vigili cum *fele* peric'lum.

This does their passion, grief, and anger raise,
And kindles the warm nation to a blaze;
They tear and rave, and o'er the mountains run,
Fly to all places, but at ease in none.
For, as old bards have in their verses sung,
The *Cambrian* hearts with wrath are quickly stung,
As if their souls, so wondrous prone to ire,
Were ting'd with brimstone, and as soon took fire.
　　Nettled alike, how all consent to shed
Their bloody vengeance on the cursed head
Of the vile caitiff; how they might ensnare
The wary robber, was their prudent care.
Long they debated on the surest course,
Or secret stratagem, or open force;
And what brave captain should their army lead,
And quell the monster in extremest need,
The conquering *cat*, who many battles won,
By whom the race was *only not undone*,
Was now deem'd useless; tho' the us'd to keep
A wakeful guard, and nigh his fastness creep,
Or watch his cavern with pretended sleep.
In vain the thief, behind his lines immur'd,
Was by his native littleness secur'd.
This was his bulwark, and from hence he draws
A strong advantage on more potent claws.
For if by chance he smelt the *centry*'s face,
Backward he slunk to his retiring place,
Unpassable by stern *Grimalkin*'s race.
Nor with new sallies ventur'd out his head,
'Till danger with the watchful pyrate fled.
Safe in his harbour, 'till the coast was clear,

Sic *Cambri* (*Cambros* liceat componere muri)
Elusere hostes, cùm *Julius*, orbe subacto,
Imperio adjecit *Britonas*; sic nempè recessit
Ad latebras gens tota, & inexpugnabile vallum,
Montes; sic sua saxa inter, medioque ruinæ
Delituit tuta, & desperans vincere, vinci
Noluit; hinc priscos memorant longo ordine *patres*,
Indomitasque crepant terras, linguæque senectam.

Felinos igitur postquam *mus* sæpius ungues
Fugerat, & *Britoni* spes non erat ulla saluties
A socio belli, supremo in limite terræ
Concilium accitur, quâ nunc *Menevia* plorat
Curatos mitræ titulos, & nomen inane
Semi sepultæ urbis; properant hinc inde frequentes
Patresque, proceresque, & odorum *sulphure* vulgus.

Tum senior, coi fæpè fuis in montibus *bircus*
Prolixam invidit barbam, cuique ora manusque
Prisca incrustavit *scabies*, spectabilis aulâ
Stat mediâ, fractus senio, *postique* reclinis
Cambrorum vexato humeries; & gutture ab imo
Densas præcipitans voces, non, "inquit, aperto

Which help'd his courage, and secur'd his fear.
     So when great CÆSAR kept the world in awe,
And *Britain* yielded to the *Roman* law,
(If custom the comparison allows
Of great with small, a *Welshman* with a *mouse*)
The *Welsh* intrench'd, to run the last of ills,
And burrough'd in their known impervious hills.
To nature's rampires the whole nation flocks,
And skulks behind impenetrable rocks.
Despair compell'd them oft to quit the field;
They could not conquer, and they would not yield.
Hence of CADWALLADARS, and a long row
Of ancestors, some thousand years ago,
They vaunt, as Heralds born, and proudly boast
Their ancient language, and unconquer'd coast.
     Since then the *mouse* with adversary guiles
Had oft out-general'd *Grimalkin*'s wiles;
And *Cambria* could no farther hope descry
Or from the claws, or craft of her ally:
A parliament is summon'd to appear
And meet in council on the land's frontier.
Where now *St David*'s, once a noble name,
Mourns her lost titles, and diminish'd fame:
Hither the fathers, lords, and mob repair
And strong with brimstone scent the ambient air.
     At this full congress an old sage appear'd
With hoary head, and venerable beard,
Envy'd by goats, which on the mountains graze;
His hands all o'er incrusted, and his face
Foul with the known distemper of the place.
Worn out with years, he on a post reclin'd,

" De cello, sed furto agitur; non exterus hostis,
" Sed majus graviusque malum, nimis intimus hospes,
" Compulit huc populum; dominabitur usq; tyrannus
" Mus petulans? Vos, ergo patres, venerabilis ordo,
" Quêis patriæ pretiofa salus, finite dolores
" Consilio tantos, & si spes ulla supersit,
" Propitias adhibete manus: sic *Cadwaladeri*
" Duna clarescat hones, vestia hîc quoq; gloria crescet.

Dixit, & ante oculous fragmenta, & mucida tollens
Frustula, relliquias furti, monumenta rapinæ,
Exacuit *Cambrorum* iras: nunc æmulus ardor
Vindictæ, nunc laudis amor, sub pectore *patrum*
Ardet, inauditam meditatur quisque ruinam
Muri, muscipulamq; statim extudit omne cereberum.

Which Cambrian shoulders often us'd to grind,
Unloaded the resentment of his mind.
He turn'd his whiskers with a graceful stroke,
And in deep tone, thus the grave father spoke.
" We're not assembled to provide relief
" 'Gainst open foes, but a clandestine thief:
" No fierce invader from some foreign part,
" But lodg'd and harbour'd in the country's heart:
" The barb'rous tyrant rages where he please,
" And, absolute, invades our lorded cheese.
" O woe! O grief of griefs! O gallant shame
" To the try'd valour of the *Cambrian* name!
" Shall we obey a saucy mouse, whose rules
" Are absolute, and made for passive fools:
" No—let it ne'er be said—but let us try
" Our force, and conquer in the cause, or die.
" Grave senators, and venerable peers,
" Your country's sword and shield, remove our fears.
" If any hope or remedy be left,
" Unite, and combat with the growing theft:
" So shall your arms our ancient fame renew,
" And brave CADWALLARS revive in you.
  He said, and then exposing to their fight
Half-eaten relicks of the tyrant's spite;
Trophies of raping, which too sure betray
How by the dint of teeth he forc'd his way,
And printed conquest on his mouldy prey.
This stings the blood, this blows the raging fire,
And with new fuel feeds the Cambrian are.
This in their hearts does emulation breed,
Some dire revenge, and some th' heroic deed,

At quidam ante alios notus cognomine *Taffi*,
Et magis ingenio celebris, cui *Wallia* nunquam
Æqualem peperit, *faber* idem, idemque *senator*,
" Eximius, sic orsus erat; si gloria gentis
" *Caseus* intereat, metuo ne tota colonum
" Deficiat cœna, & *mensæ* decus omne *secundæ*
" Divitibus pereat; quoniam ergo *Wallica* virtus,
" Et feles nequeant superare hæc monstra, fabrilis
" Dextera quid possit, quid machina parva, dolique
" Experiar; *dolus, an virtus, quis in hoste requirit?*

Talia jactantem circumstant undique fixis
Hærentes oculis, sperataque guadia læto
Murmure certatim testantur, & unde salutem
Promissam expectent, rogitant, ardentque doceri.

In flames with thirst of glory; all contend
By various deaths to work the robber's end,
And hammer on the anvil of their brain
Incredible machines of cruel pain.
The bearded fires are on destruction bent,
And fortune labours with the vast event.
   But one above the rest was more renown'd,
TAPHY his name, than whom was never found
A smarter genius in the country round.
No Blacksmith for a senator more fit,
Surpassing all at hammer or at wit.
He wav'd the greasy profits of his trade,
Whenever injur'd WALES implor'd his aid.
In words, like these, the brave illustrious man
Attack'd his audience, and he thus began;
" Fathers and brethren, if the fame decrease
" Of our rich morsels, and our envy'd cheese,
" The hungry ploughman will most damage feel,
" And lose at supper a substantial meal.
" The wealthy too will have a loser's share,
" And crown no banquets with the dainty fare,
" Since they nor we are able to withstand
" The salvage monsters which infest the land;
" Since not Grimalkin's strength, nor fraud prevail,
" I'll try, if this right hand, this head will fail.
" 'Tis all the fame, if with success we meet,
" Whether we gain by valour or deceit.
   This strikes the reverend council with surprize;
They gape, and stare, and listen with their eyes
A sudden joy does every heart dilate
In silent wishes for their better fate,

Ille caput scalpens, (nam multùm scalpere *Cambris*
Expedit) horrendum subrisit, & ora resolvens
Talia verba refert. "Cum sessus membra quieti
" Hesternâ sub nocte dedi, sopor obmit altus
" Lumina, mus audax sectatus, opinor, odores
" Quos non concoctas pingui exhalavit ab ore
" *Caseus*, accessit furtim, & compage solutis
" Faucibus irrepsit, jamque ipsa in viscera lapsus,
" Crudas ventris opes rapere, hesternamque paravit
" Heu! malè munito furari è gutture cœnam.
" Excussus subitò somnis, sub dente latronem,
" Dum refilire parat, prenfi, fruftráque rebellem ·
" Mordaci vinc'lo astrinxi. Sic carcere murem
" Posse capi infructus, nova mox ergaftula, mecum
" Hæc meditans, fatui fabricare, animoque catenas
" Effinxi tales, mihi quas suggesserat oris
" Captivus. Mirum O! quali regit omnia lege
" Dextra arcana *Jovis!* Quam cæcis passibus errat
" Causarum series! nobis mus ipse salutem
" Invitus dedit, & quos attulit ante dolores,
" Tollere jam docuit; neve hunc habuisse magistrum
" Vos pudeat, *patres*; *fas est vel ab hoste doceri.*

To know the means they earnestly desire,
And what, and when, and where, and how inquire?
　　Then TAPHY scratch'd his head, a pleasure grown
Familiar to the *Cambrian* clime alone.
He grinn'd a horrid laugh, and thus he said;
" When yester night had caft her silent shade,
" And me surrender'd to refreshing deep,
" Which on my limbs and eyes began to creep:
" A mouse audacious follow'd by degrees
" The fumy steams of unconcocted cheese,
" Which from my mouth I threw; the pyrate leap'd
" Thro' my unguarded jaws, and down the flipp'd
" Into my bowels, and began to prey
" On th' undigested meals of yesterday.
" But while his way the thief returning fought,
" I snapt him, and betwixt my grinders caught;
" Wak'd from my sleep at some surprizing thought;
" In vain the rebel struggled, and in vain
" Us'd his poor strength to break the biting chain,
" This hint, at last, revolving in my mind,
" How mice might be subdu'd, if once confin'd;
" The notions crouded in my teeming head,
" And a new prison and new fetters made,
" From such a model fashion'd and dispos'd,
" As the late captive of my teeth inclos'd.
" O wond'rous! by what art, what secret springs
" The hand of Jove moves sublunary things!
" How nature does a constant tenour keep!
" And what effects from unthought causes leap!
" Th' instructive mouse has taught us now to save
" Our cheese, and make the conqueror a slave,

Hæc ubi dicta, domum repetit, comitantur euntem
Plaudentes populi, atque benigna laboribus optant
Omina. Tam celeri sua quisque ad limina cursu
Nuncius is, laribusque refert, que munera Taffi
Ingenio speranda forent; dumque ordine narrant
Omnia, dumque deis, ut tanta inccepta secundent,
Vota ferunt, monitæ præsago pectore felés,
Plus solito lusere, & (si fas credere famæ)
Sub manibus matrum saliere coagula lactis.

Intereà Taffi manibufque animoque vicissim
Instat magno operi, & divinâ Palladis arte
Muscipulam ædificat; fit machina mira, novâque
Induitur valtûs specie tragi-comica moles.

Quin age, si tibi, Musa, vacat, spectacula pandas
Infantis fabricæ, & percurrens singula, totam
Compagem expedias. Quadrati lamina ligni
Summum imumque tegit, filorum ferreus ordo

" And tho' unwilling cures the wounds he gave.
" Nor blush, grave Sires, that to a mouse you owe
" The stratagem to work his overthrow;
" 'Tis wife to take instructions from a foe.
 This said, the congress rofe, and TAPHY strait
To his respective home repairs in state:
Peals of applause from the attending throng
Wounded the *Æther*, as he past along.
The tattling nurses spread abroad his fame,
And lisping infants stammer out his name:
All full of TAPHY, none but TAPHY sing,
What wonders from his mighty wit would spring
How great the nation's *better hope* would grow
By conquering an hereditary foe.
But while they offer up their prayers, to bless
His brain's ingenious issue with success,
Lo! wond'rous to behold! the sober cat,
Who by the fire but now demurely fat,
Brick as a kitling, twirl'd her boding tail,
And, if the faith of poets may prevail,
The curds were seen to dance within the milking pail.
 Mean time with tooth and nail, with hand and brain,
Did TAPHY, like another VULCAN, strain;
While PALLAS help'd him with her art and oil,
To finish his divine, laborious toil,
A MOUSE-TRAP call'd, nor heard before, nor seen,
A wond'rous *tragi-comical* machine.
 And now, my Muse, do thou vouchsafe to smile,
Describe this fabric in no vulgar tile,
And paint the nicest parts of the stupendous pile;
In form quadrangular two planks are laid,

Munit utrumque latus, parvisque uti fulta columnis
Stat domus; introitus patet insidiosus, amicum
Muribus hospitium ostentans; sed desuper horret
Janua, perniciem minitans, tenuique ruina
Suspensa est silo; (usque adeò sua stamina *Paræ*
Muribus intexunt, & pendent omnia filo.)
In summo tecti, mediâque in parte tabellæ,
Stat lignum, erectum, scisso cum vertice, cui trabs
Parvula transverfim inseritur, juftèque libratas
Utrinque extendit palmas, quarum altera quantùm
Deprimitur, tantùm annexam levat altera portam.
Interiore domo, per tecti exile foramen
Demissum pendet ferrum, quod mobile ludit
Hùc illùc facili tactu; curvatur in hamum
Infima pars, escamque tenet; pars altera prendit
Perfidiosa trabem extremam, at cum senferit hostem
Lethales guftâste cibos, mora nulla, solutam
Dimittit portam, primumque ulciscitur ictum.

MUSCIPULA

One founds the basis, and one crowns the head,
The sides around are fortify'd with wires,
On which strong columns the whole house aspires
An entry does insidiously entice
With hospitable look the pilgrim *mice*:
But from above depends a threat'ning board,
Hung by a twine, like DAMOCLES's sword.
(So all are serv'd by Fates, who weave the doom
Of mice and men upon one common loom!)
High on the surface of the fabrick stands
A pole, on whose notch'd head a beam expands
It's wooden arms, and pois'd alike in all;
One end mounts upwards by the other's fall.
Within the dome a slender wire depends,
Which from the top thro' a small hole descends,
Which pendulously wantons here and there,
And at the slightest touch plays loose in air.
The lower part a hook, portending fate,
But flesh'd and brib'd with an alluring bait:
The upper part does treacherously seem
To bite with iron tooth: the extreamest beam;
But soon as she has felt the nibbling foe,
She drops her hold, and lets the portal go:
There, without bail or main-prize, or relief,
She shops for life (too short!), the greedy thief.
Thus far, has TAPHY play'd the builder's part,
A pile erected by the rules of art.
But now to furnish his enchanted house,
And kill with kindness the devoted mouse;
In flames he fortifies the scented bait,
And loads the cheating hook with luscious fate.

His itâ dispofitis, pendentem protinùs hamum
Induitinfidiis *Taffi*, exitiosaque *muri*
Ipsa alimenta facit, sed quo fragrantior esset.
Caseus, & *murem* invitaret longiùs, escam
Fatalem torret flammis, vimque addit odori.

Et jam nox memoranda aderat, cùm feffa cubili
Membra levans *Taffi*, juxta pulvinar amicam
Muscipulam statuit, fidoque satellite tutus
Indulsit facili somno, Gens improba, *mures*
Lascivi intereà exiliant, noctisque silentis
Præsidio confisi errant; tum naribus acer
Mus quidam, dux eximius, diis natus iniquis,
Castra inimica petit, quò grato flamine tostus
Caseus allexit. Venienti prima resistunt
Clathra, aditumq; negant: sed turpem ferre repulsam
Ille indignatus, munimina ferrea circum
Cursitar, & crispat nasum, introitumque sagaci
Explorat barbâ; jamque irremeabile limen
Ingressus, votique potens, tristem arripit escam,
Exitiumque vorat lætus, potiturque ruinâ.

And now was come the memorable night,
Design'd to do the suffering *Cambrians* right.
Down on his bed undaunted TAPHY lay,
And in soft slumbers lost the toils of day;
The friendly engine near his pillow kept
A faithful guard, while the bold hero slept:
Mean time the mice, a frisking nation, play'd,
Protected by the night's officious shade.
A mouse of high degree did first expose
His valiant life in quest of prey, and foes,
Of sharpest teeth, and most sagacious nose.
But vain's our courage, if a luckless sign
With beams malignant on our cradle shine;
Or if a mouse of hopeful parts be torn,
Grimalkin's victim, and a *Welshman's* scorn.
   Up strait the leader march'd, his prey to seize;
For to his nostrils some auspicious breeze
Had borne the grateful scent of toasted cheese.
But wiry pallisades impeach his way,
And the first onset of his fury stay,
Yet his great soul a vile repulse disdains,
And double vigour from resistance gains;
With curling nose and searching beard explores
An entrance at th' inexorable doors,
Which upward held, the willing guest admit
To taste his ruin in the savoury bit;
Then dropping downwards with a frightful sound,
Th' unhappy captain of the mice surround.

Taffi, exaudito strepitu, quem pendola porta
Lapsa dedit, cubito erigitur thalamoque triumphans
Exilit, impatiens discendi, quis novus hospes
Venerat. Intereà furit intùs *ridiculus mus*,
Et fronte, & pedibus pugnat, jamque intervallis
Clathrorum capat impingit ferrumque fatigat
Dentibus infanis. Sic olim in retia *Marsus*
Actus aper, fremit horrendus, sinuosaque quassat:
Vincula, ludibrium catulis, diffusa per armos
It spuma, arrectæque rigent in pectore setæ.

Postera lux *oritur*, decurrunt montibus altis
Præcipites *Cambri*, nam cunctas venit ad aure
Res nova; quippe *asinus*, solitâ gravitate remissa
Et jam pigritiæ oblitus, lascivior *hædo*
Ascendít montem, quâ *Cambrum*, dissonas ore,
Præconem simulans, ter rauco gutture rudens,
Te celebrat, *Taffi*, ter publica narrat amicis
Gaudia. *Bubo* etiam (*Cambrorum* dictus ab illo
Tempore *Legatus*) per compita ubique, per urbes,
Totâ nocte errans, rostrum ferale fenestris
Stridulus impegit, cecinitque instantia muri
Funera. *Parturiunt montes*; atque agmine denso
Penbrochiæ multus ruit incola, *Merviniæque*;
Quique tenent *Bonium*, & *Mariduni* mœnia vate
Inclyta *Merlino*; veniunt fœcunda *Glamorgan*

Muscipula

The sudden noise rous'd Taphy from repose,
Who at the call of victory arose:
He burns impatiently to know, and learn
This new adventure of a high concern.
Mean time the mouse, his conquest, raves within,
And bounces in th' irrefragable gin.
New to his prison, and new fashion'd hold,
He fumes and stamps, like Bajazet of old,
His head against the slender bars he beats,
And with mad teeth th' impassive iron eats:
So when a hunter toils a *Marsian* boar,
The woods rebellow with his hideous roar;
The youth around his idle tusks deride,
The sport of mastiff, who afflict his side:
His useless foam he on his shoulders throws,
And on his back a bristly forest grows.
   The morning sun discovers to the fight
The triumphs of the Trap, and silent night.
From their steep mountains the swift *Cambrians* run,
And with huzza's proclaim the battle won.
The ass, an enemy to toil and pain,
Had chang'd his nature to a merry vein:
Frisk'd like a kid, and like a lambkin play'd,
And thrice the publick joy he loudly bray'd:
Thee, Taphy, thrice he roars to hills around,
Thee, Taphy, thrice the echoing hills resound.
The hooting owl (since that auspicious time
Declar'd the *Herald* of the *Cambrian* clime)
All night through open streets and cities flew,
And his presaging beak against the windows threw:
Loudly he rang from his unluckly throat

Quos alit, & *Vagæ* potor, rigidusque colonus
Gomerici montis. Tum, circumstante coronâ,
Illudit capto *Taffi*, iratumque lacessens,
" *Nequicquam lucteris*, (ait) *damnaberis aræ*
" *Victima prima mea, memorique bæc limina tinges*
" *Sanguine; spes nulla est, retrò fugientibus obstant*
" *Non exorandi postes: dabis, improbe, pœnas*
" *Pro meritis, vitamque simul cum carcere linques.*

Vix ea fatus erat, cù ludicra *felis* aprico
Culmine defiliit tecti, quò sæpe solebat,
Cruribus extensis, molli languescere luxu.
Aspicit instantem captivus, & erigit aures,
Gibbosoque riget tergo, nec limen apertum
Jam tentare audet, sed in ipso carcere solam
Spem libertatis ponens, sua vincula prensat
Unguibus hamatis, pedibusque tenacibus hæret.
Excutitur tamen; & *felis* rapidissima prædæ

The captive's fatal knell with dismal note.
The mountains travel, and from *Pembroke* come
A clan of tenants, from *Mervina*[1] some:
Some colonies from *Maridunum*[2] throng,
Renown'd for MERLIN in the *British* song.
With those who dwell nigh mitred *Bangor*'s walls,
And those, where *Vaga* into *Severn* falls;
With those who climb *Montgomery*'s steep hill,
Or fruitful vallies of *Glamorgan* till.
Then TAPHY with sarcastic voice exults,
And thus the raging little slave insults:
" In vain, vile caitiff, dost thou tear and rend,
" And at the bar of destiny contend:
" In vain with stamping feet and teeth assail,
" Nor with thy boasted littileness prevail.
" Remember now, thy thefts and plunders all
" Start up in judgment, and for vengeance call.
" In vain you seek just punishment to fly,
" Those bars all hopes of an escape deny.
" No! wicked victim, thou art doom'd to bleed,
" And with thy blood this floor, this altar feed;
" And may all rav'nous mice, like thee, succeed!
    He said, and *puss*, who the proceedings spy'd,
Leap'd from a neighbouring roof's warm sunny side,
Where the was wont to bask, and wear away
In luxury and ease a summer's day.
The captive mouse had kenn'd her from afar,
And now intent to shun the coming war,
He seeks no flight, but more improv'd in fears,

---

1   Merionetshire.

2   Carmarthen.

Involat, & frustrà luctantem evadere sævo
Implicat amplexu, crudeliaque oscula figit.
Nulla datur requies; agili sinuamine caudæ
Gaudia testatur victrix, & flexile corpus
Lascivio versans faltu, modò corpore prono
Attentè invigilat muri, modò colla benignis
Unguiculis levitèr palpans, mentitur amorem
Dum lacerare parat; variâ sic arte jocosam
Barbariem exercet, lapidâque tyrannide ludit.

At nugis tandem defessa, nec ampliùs iram
Dissimulans, acuit dentes, &, more leonis
Impasti, incumbit prædæ: jam pectore ab imo
Murmurat, & tremulos artus, & sanguine sparsa
Viscera dilaniat. Plebs circumfusa cruorem
Invisum aspiciens, lætis clamoribus implent
Æthera; clamoresque Echo, *Cambræ* incola terræ,
Læta refert; resonant *Plinlimmonis* ardua moles,
Et *Brechin*, & Snowdon; vicina ad sidera fertur
Plausus, & ingenti strepit *Offa fossa* tumultu.

Tu, Taffi, æternùm vives; tua munera *Cambri*

152

Bristles his crumpled back, and pricks his ears;
To scape the stern devouring *mouser*'s jaws,
His hope of safety from his prison draws,
And hugs his fetters with tenacious claws:
But all in vain; for puss expecting lay
With nimble feet to seize her panting prey;
On whom, when shaken from his holds, she flies,
And fixes cruel kisses on her prize.
She tells what secret joys within prevail,
By wanton motions of her twirling tail.
Sometimes she, careless, on the ground reclines,
Still watchful on her captive's dark designs;
Sometimes the paws his neck, and licks his face,
And girds him with a barbarous embrace:
With sportive cruelty, a subtle task,
She acts the tyrant in a lover's mask.
    But now the merry scene of action's past,
And, like an unfed lioness, at last,
Tir'd with her wanton play, and trifling toil,
She growls and grumbles o'er her trembling spoils;
And while his bowels and his limbs she rends,
Loud acclamations to the clouds ascends.
Echo, the tenant of the *Cambrian* hills,
With the repeated shout the caverns fills.
Brechin, and *Snowdon*, and *Plinlimmon*'s mount,
And *Offa*'s ditch the various toils recount:
Resound the fortune of their country's wars,
Their Naughter'd tyrant, and their finish'd jars,.
And bear the triumph to the neighb'ring stars.

    But thou, O TAPHY, in my verse shalt live

Nunc etiam celebrant, quotiesque revolvitur annus,
Te memorant; patrium gens grata tuetur honorem,
Festivoque ornat redolentia tempora PORRO.

FINIS

The long eternity which Poets give.
The Welsh with annual joy preserve thy fame,
Thou brightest honour of the Cambrian name!
Thy country does with gratitude o'erflow,
And tho' no conquering bays she can bestow,
Yet fragrant leeks shall for thy brows, instead of
   laurel grow.

The END

Index